CW00815858

From 1 to 85

Kenneth Nixon

First published in Great Britain by Pen Press

All paper used in the printing of this book has been made from wood
grown in managed, sustainable forests.

ISBN13: 978-1-907499-01-2

Printed and bound in the UK
Pen Press is an imprint of Indepenpress Publishing Limited
25 Eastern Place
Brighton
BN2 1GJ

A catalogue record of this book is available from
the British Library

Cover design by Jacqueline Abromeit

Acknowledgements

Mrs Cowey – A teacher who I never really knew. She must have seen a spark of some sort in me and gave me a chance.

S.S. Mooltan – This rusty old tub probably saved my life by breaking down while rounding the Cape in 1941.

Fred Griffith – We taught together for twenty years and had so much in common. A shame that he died after so little retirement as he deserved more.

Jo Nixon – Just for putting up with me for over fifty years.

Prologue

When I reached the age of eighty five and because of impending illness I decided to write a life history. The first ongoing years seemed to divide nicely into five year compartments so I decided to carry this through for seventeen five year eras.

The main reason for doing this at all was to give me something to do. I hope it will be of some interest to my fairly large family.

One to Five

My twin sister and I were six weeks old when our father died. He had been wounded during the Gallipoli campaign in the First World War and had suffered from septicaemia and never really recovered. Well, that was what my mother told us when we were old enough to understand but I often wondered if the shock of producing twins had something to do with his demise. At the time my eldest brother Leslie was ten years old, my second brother Gordon was eight and my elder sister Doreen was six so suddenly my Mother was left with quite a problem. Five in fact.

We were born in Wellhall Road in Eltham Kent and my earliest memories are of a wooden bungalow which was the pre-fab of the time, comfortable and warm and quite roomy. It was one of a long row of such buildings which probably housed other army families. They were built on brick pillars and I remember as a child playing games by crawling underneath.

There is no doubt that we were poor. My mother had some form of army pension! I remember her telling me that our father's name had been added to the war memorial in Eltham, as having died for his country and I have thought of visiting it in my later life but never got round to going there. My elder brothers did paper rounds, not I might add for personal gain but to augment our family income.

The earliest recollection that I can put a date to happened when sister Viv and I went to school at three and a half years old. We were born on May 20th 1921 so that is easy to work out. Mother had been allowed special dispensation to send us to school at that age because she needed to work part time to give us a reasonable life style.

I can still remember the smell of that classroom because it had an impregnated atmosphere of chalk. The other thing that lingers on is the horrible noise made by slate pencils on the wooden edged slates that we had to use. Beyond that I cannot remember too much about that school.

Our amusements were very simple as we made our own, we didn't seem to get into much trouble but I can remember one occasion when we were not very popular with Mum. At the end of the road was a long grassy hill that had probably been left after the builders had excavated for the bungalows. It was quite high, thirty or forty feet with a sloping end and some of the other children had devised a mud ski-ride. On a wet day with the aid of a tin tray (very popular in those days) you could run towards the sloping end and jump on the tray and whizz for about thirty or forty yards with considerable momentum. Of course Viv and I decided to try this one day, Mum being out and two metal trays available. It was great fun but repeated rides had turned the slide into a veritable quagmire with disastrous results. I can still visualise Viv at four years old with her pretty short dress and flying pigtails careering down this slide. As you can imagine Mum was not amused at the sight of two very muddied siblings. She did have a sense of humour but well hidden on this occasion I expect.

The bungalow that we lived in was at the end of the row and next to it set in an elevated position was the first house. The occupants were a Mr and Mrs Holland who were a kindly middle aged couple and I suspect kindly disposed towards my Mother's predicament. On some Saturdays I was for some reason, invited to have tea with them. This was an occasion and I was suitably polished and dressed for it and I must say rather honoured.

This completes my recollections of those early days. What surprises me is how feeble one's memory can be, for example, my eldest brother would have been fifteen when we left Eltham and have left school but I can't remember what his employment was! Somehow, we travelled from Eltham to rural Suffolk but I can't remember how! Could we have gone by train from London to Ipswich? Too far to have done it by horse and cart! Road transport was not a likely option in 1926. Perhaps we left a lot of stuff behind and went by train. Anyway it should have been an exciting journey for a five year old boy but I cannot remember doing it.

Five to Ten

When my mother remarried in 1926 she was in fact returning to her roots. The house we were to live in was semi-detached and situated in an area of trees with a garden area of about half an acre. Her parents lived next door, her elderly father bedridden with arthritis but her mother a wiry tough lady of considerable spirit and character. Mother's new husband whom she had known when a schoolgirl was ten years her junior and you would think a brave man to have taken on such a large task. His name was Percy Wayman and a man of medium size but quite strong and wiry. He had worked at Stannay Farm all his life and had been promoted to head horseman and in truth was very good at his job. The farm was situated about half a mile from our new house. To get to it you had to walk across heathland to the farm. The fields and agricultural area became Bentwaters aerodrome in the war. The farm house was quite large and prosperous by all accounts.

For me as a five year old child it was amazing to be transported from a drab urban street in outer London to a countryside wonderland in rural Suffolk. It was early in the year at springtime when the wild life was beginning to bloom. To me it seemed so exciting and different: to see small rabbits running around in the heathland and to hear the birds singing was truly exhilarating. Our new house geographically was at the end of Friday Street and Viv and I had to walk to Rendlesham to get to school. Having left the treed areas we walked along a sandy lane with shack type dwellings scattered along the sides. This eventually became a narrow road with bungalows and houses about and then Rendlesham itself. A quiet little village with a shop, church school etc which during the next four years we were to get to know quite well. My elder brother and I visited Rendlesham on a nostalgic journey after the Second World War. We went down Friday Street and found little change and the house still in the trees, one side still lived in, the other in a dilapidated run down condition. We took a photograph of the old place which I still have.

I got on quite well with my step father but my elder siblings, because they had known our own father were not so enamoured with the new regime. They of course accepted the situation for our mother's sake and for the five years we were in Suffolk things went along fairly harmoniously. Lesley at fifteen had a job in a biscuit factory at Hadleigh, and he was allowed to eat as many biscuits as he wanted. For the rest of his life he just hated biscuits but at the time we did benefit because he was allowed to bring broken biscuits home from time to time.

Gordon had also left school and worked with our step father on the farm. He was a more robust lad than Leslie and was often called Hector because of his bullying tendencies. In colouring both he and elder sister Doreen favoured our mother having dark hair and brown eyes but we twins and eldest son Leslie were fair with blue eyes like our father. Gordon was good at the work and seemed to enjoy working with the large shire horses of the time. He was taught how to plough but I remember him best at grass mowing with a semi mechanical mower. It had a horizontal reciprocating blade that was geared to the wheels and as he drove the horse forward it cut a clean swathe down the meadow. The grass was grown specially for animal fodder, an important part of farming in those days. Another horse pulled rakes, put the grass into rows when it was dry and the final more boring job of stacking the hay had to be done by hand. I can still remember the huge knife type tool that was used to slice lumps of the hay when needed during the winter months to feed the numerous animals.

My sister Doreen was a gem for the whole of her life and especially to me during darker times of my life. When we arrived in Suffolk she went to school at Tunstall for a few terms. Tunstall was a larger village about four miles from our house and she had to walk there as I and our younger sister did when we had progressed from the junior school at Rendlesham. On leaving school she went into service at Rendlesham Lodge which was housed in a walled estate with a forbidding large door that always seemed to be closed. She "lived in", as was the expression of the time, and we didn't seem to see much of her. I don't remember her making any fuss at her lot and in truth she had that stoic attitude to life always. She was quite an attractive girl with wavy brown hair and an honest way about her that she carried on throughout her life.

The only thing that my twin sister and I had in common was that we were born at the same time. Throughout our lives she always claimed that she had the looks and the fun while I had the brains and a dull existence. She was probably right about that as she certainly led the lads of her acquaintance a merry dance.

One day when we were about eight years old and when I had purloined a packet of Wills woodbines from brother Gordon we decided to light up on the way to school. That cigarette was the first and last that I indulged in as I was terribly sick (lucky for me). She continued to smoke for the rest of her life and died of a lung related disease in her late seventies. She did eventually settle down to a sedentary life with husband Ron but theirs being a war time marriage, they had problems that were very usual in war time.

I look back on those fine years in Suffolk with great affection. We had real weather in those days with beautiful springs and summers but a gradual hardening as winter approached through autumn. To have snow falls of five feet thick or more was quite common and tended to be that way for several months. Transport was difficult and shank's pony had to prevail. Our long galvanised bath did double duty at these times as we often tied a rope to the end handle, filled it with commodities such as firewood, coal, groceries etc and towed it through the snow. This worked quite well and was a fun full achievement. The bath which was about five foot long still did its other duty for the Friday night scrub in front of a roaring fire.

It was on one such occasion that this roaring fire caused the chimney to ignite! The fire used to be fuelled with wood usually as coal was very expensive and chimney sweeping often neglected. One of the brothers came in to say that flames were shooting out of the brick chimney which was quite worrying as the top part of the house was wooden boarded. Why I remember this so vividly is because for once in her life my mother panicked.

She simply gathered her most precious item, a second hand fur coat, and ran from the house. I remember her sitting under a large tree with the coat draped around her. Fortunately the fire burned itself out and all was well but it was a very scary time for us all.

About this time when I was about eight we acquired a mode of transport. The farmer had a high spirited young pony intended only as a pony for one of their children. When the pony proved unsuitable for the purpose he actually *gave* it to step father Perce. He spent a lot of time and patience with the animal and eventually schooled it well enough to pull a second hand trap that he somehow acquired. Perce and mother soon began to use this transport for leisure runs and things appeared to be going well.

One Saturday it was decided to go by trap to a local horse show and ploughing match. Now, the trap consisted roughly of a box with four upholstered corner seats with a door at the rear end and a metal step at the back to step up on. The axle containing the wheels was bolted to the box and the shafts for the pony with various hooks for the harness was also part of the sub frame attached to the box cabin.

Perce, Mother, Gordon and I were to be the passengers on this day. I can remember being dressed in my best and being suitably polished and stood to one side! Gordon was also ready and in his jacket and breeches looking very much the part. He and Perce harnessed the horse and Gordon stood at the pony's head while Mum and Step Dad readied themselves for the trip.

What happened next still makes me shudder with apprehension. Someone at the back of the trees fired a shot gun (not an uncommon thing in those days when people lived off the land.) The pony reared up on its hind legs and bolted. How the wheels missed Gordon I don't know. Perhaps the rearing part gave him a second to throw himself clear but it was so close to being a tragic event.

The pony with trap was initially going towards Friday Street but the disturbed animal decided to enter through the end garden gate which was open. The pony got through but the trap didn't as it was too wide at the wheels resulting in the wheels and axle being torn apart with disastrous results.

I don't think my parents ever realised how narrow an escape Gordon had, but I was standing by, probably with my finger in my mouth and saw it all. That was the end of our transport era. I cannot tell what happened to the pony as I never saw it again. Things were very harsh in those days so I expect it would have been destroyed.

The half acre garden was very productive and we were quite self sufficient with quite a good labour force provided by the family. The soil was really wonderful for growing. Being under the trees helped and with the occasional load of horse manure from the farm the potential was excellent. Most of the plot was set with potatoes and this was where I came in! Perce set some suitable potatoes aside for seed each year and some of these I remember were sliced in two if they were large. The setting method was simple as a string was fixed across the plot as a guide and he just put his spade in the soil creating a slot and I carrying a bucket of seed potatoes dropped a potato or half into the slot. He then withdrew the spade and stamped the ground level. Simple! I think that harvesting the potatoes was an even bigger thrill as when they were ready in the spring a light forking would bring the new potatoes to the surface. Usually there was a wonderful crop and afterwards you could still see the old half potato and wonder how it could have produced such sweet and enjoyable food. Other produce from that garden was equally good and we certainly got a good reward for our labours.

Our water supply was a deep well with the usual bucket and rope attachment to raise the water. The top part was brick and had a wooden cover which was about five feet above the ground and quite safe. We used the water as it came from the well and I am sure we never boiled it. We seemed to thrive very well on this and were healthy enough. I cannot remember ever going near a doctor during these times which speaks for itself.

About this time my mother's father died. He had been bedridden for years worn out by the hard life he had lived probably on the same farm. I don't remember ever seeing him, which now seems strange, but I can remember him being referred to as 'old ninety' so I guess he was very old. He just didn't figure in my life as a grandfather and that is how it was.

Our maternal grandmother was quite different. I can still see her strutting off with her two shopping baskets to walk the five miles to Wickham Market. She was a tough lady, quite tall and brisk in everything she did. She did this each week on market days whatever the weather and brought all the necessary perquisites back. This I suppose would have included coal tar soap for toilet purposes, huge bars of sunlight soap for hand washing the clothes etc. We didn't have many luxury items I'm sure but jam, eggs, and some fruit would have been part of the purchases.

The home grown food we had including fruit from the trees had a special taste. Tomatoes had a wonderful aroma and richness that one never gets from supermarket shelves of today and that was true of other things such as broad beans, peas and other common food items. The farmer grew turnips in those days for animal food also mangel-wurzel and other beets. We often raided the fields when the turnips were young and when cooked, mashed and mixed with margarine made a very tasty vegetable. Of course rabbit meat played a big part of our diet and also an occasional game bird. Stepfather was allowed to have a twelve-bore shot gun to keep down vermin which included the numerous rabbits on the heath. His father was head gamekeeper on the Bentwater estate which extended beyond the farm. This area during World War Two was taken over and became a massive base for the American army air force. It is still a concrete jungle to this day but I don't know what its purpose is now.

Percy's mother and father were both short and rather portly people. I remember him in his tweed gamekeeper's garb with his deerstalker hat and he was rarely seen without his broken shot gun under his arm. He had an important job and took it very seriously. Pheasants, partridges and other game birds whether young or old were in his charge and woe behold any predators whether four legged or two legged that threatened his charges. They lived in a cottage at the end of Rendlesham Forest and he used to hang up the vermin which included birds such as rooks, crows, stoats, weasels or anything else that endangered the young game birds or eggs, on wires hung between stakes. This was partly to ward off other dangerous creatures but during hot or warm weather created an awful smell.

Viv and I changed school at eight years which meant going to the senior school at Tunstall. By road this was a four mile walk but there was an option, which was to go cross country. This took us across the heath and by Stannay farm along the edge of Rendlesham Forest which would bring us to Tunstall by the back door route which measured just over three miles. Being quite strong and sturdy we used the second way whenever possible. This route took us by my stepfather's parents house and his mother used to invite us in. She was a jolly well rounded lady who was very kind. On occasions especially in cold weather she would invite us in for a warm up and if it was a baking day we would be given a buttered scone and a warm drink. We really looked forward to this as it was a rare treat. She made very good use of her copper which was heated beneath by a wood fire. This heated the water for general purposes but mainly for her washing, but on occasions when we went she was brewing beer in it and the hops and yeast smell was really something!

At the end of one year at Tunstall school things were about to change for us as a family. The Forestry Commission bought the heath and part of the farm to be planted with fir trees. Perce lost his job but we continued to live in the cottage for a short time while he applied for another post. By the time this happened the area was thickly populated with these small firs which were about two feet high. Today they form an extension of the Rendlesham Forest and are about forty feet high.

He got a farm job near the village of Badingham which was about ten miles from Rendlesham and four or so from the town of Framlingham. The first cottage was a run down sort of place situated on a sloping field above the main road through Framlingham to Badingham. We called these places Fram and Bad to make things a lot easier on the tongue. At the rear of the house was an ancient orchard which was as old and run down as the place itself. Nevertheless the gnarled old trees had first class fruit that year and the plums, bullaces, pears and apples were really great so that was a redeeming feature. We went to Badingham village school for about a year which meant that Viv and I had been at five different schools by the age of ten.

I was involved in a scary incident at about this time. As lads, we made pop guns by removing the central pith from a short piece of alder so you could make a tube. We made a handle from a piece of straight stick of slightly smaller diameter than this hole as pusher. If an acorn was pushed tightly into each end of the tube which was about six inches long and one acorn rammed towards the other the air pressure would blow the end acorn out at considerable force and accuracy.

Larking about after school one evening I foolishly aimed my pop gun at another boy and the acorn missile hit him in the face. He screamed and bolted home and I had a most uncomfortable evening and night expecting an irate parent seeking retribution at our door. If it had hit him in the eye it could have been very serious indeed and I realised how stupid I had been. Fortunately he appeared at school next day with just a red spot on his cheek and not greatly agitated, but from then on pop guns were out for me.

Lesley and sister Doreen continued their weary jobs during this period of time and Gordon worked on the farm with stepfather.

Somehow, we never settled in that place and its name Oaken Hill Cottage was perhaps the best part about it, except for the fruit. It is no longer there so after we left in 1931 it must have been levelled and become part of the field.

From Ten to Fifteen

In most people's lives there will no doubt be defining moments and when I look back over the past eighty-five years of my life one of these happened to me during 1931 and another in 1940. We will come to that later.

Our next home was the end one of a row of farm worker's cottages. The ones at each end were slightly larger than the middle two and as we were a family we had one of these. Perce was to be head horseman and in charge of the working horses and the family hacks. Opposite the cottages were the stables, cowsheds, piggery and various barns for storage purposes. Lesley became part of the set up and was put in charge of the poultry. This was an industry in itself as there were probably two thousand or more chickens in various stages of growth. They were heated in incubators that produced the chicks and it went on from there. The adult hen houses were situated in a large meadow surrounded by a high wire fence let into the ground to keep out the foxes and other predators. Caring for the hens, collecting the eggs and other vital chores was a full time job and Lesley used a horse to move the hen houses about. This enabled the grass to recover and keep the meadow relatively fresh. The birds were mainly Rhode Island Reds which seemed to be a good productive breed and I was warned not to go near the cockerel compound as they could be very fierce. Les seemed to enjoy this new challenge and a much healthier life than being in a biscuit factory.

The new farm was called New Buildings Farm and was two miles from the village of Great Chishill in Cambridgeshire. It meant a two mile walk to school which to us was luxury after the three plus miles set that we were used to in Suffolk. The main snag was that Viv and I were to become keen church goers and were soon inaugurated into the choir and Sunday School. The keenness was not of our making of course as this would mean walking three times to the village church on a Sunday which became quite a chore.

My elder sister Doreen was found work in the Golden Lion Hotel in Newmarket. This was twenty two miles away but as usual she seemed to settle into her new environment and made steady progress at her fresh line of work. Gordon just carried on as a general farm worker and seemed content with his lot and this state of affairs carried on for about two years of our five year stay at this farm, after which things began to change rapidly.

The village school master was quite elderly and due to retire after we had been at the school four terms. I was not one of his favourite pupils and to me he had the attitude that if one was a farm worker's child then one would remain one. There were two farmer's sons at the school and one of these had a sister who was my age. They seemed to get better treatment because of their status and I can remember resenting this. The boys themselves were friendly enough and being of a similar age we got on reasonably well.

We had a religious assembly each morning after which a central partition divided the junior section of the school from the senior part. There were about thirty pupils altogether, about half in each room, and the building was heated by a large tortoise stove. This was situated at the junior end of the building and consisted of a large cast iron tube about two feet in diameter and four feet high. It stood on four iron legs to insulate it from the floor and was fed with coke through a hinged door at the bottom or from a hinged flap at the top. A pipe went from the back of the top part up through the roof to take away the fumes. The whole thing was very efficient and was surrounded by a guard rail on which we could hang our wet outer clothing.

As said before we had real winters in those days and often arrived at school in a dishevelled state. In spite of this my favourite schoolmaster would sometimes line us up for inspection before school. His usual remark to me was that if you can't shine at one end you can shine at the other but in spite of that I would eventually have the last laugh.

There was a good general store in the village that included the Post Office. Most things could be obtained there and we were allowed a monthly account. One month Viv decided to take advantage of this by buying sweets or candy bars on the slate and not declaring some. This led to retribution at the end of the month and I remember being equally blamed in spite of my protestations. Fortunately the lady at the Post Office came to my aid in this matter but for a while relations between my sister and I were at a low.

The postmaster used a vehicle in those early days called a Trojan. It was a very noisy vehicle with three wheels. It was driven by some sort of two stroke engine by belt which went direct from the engine pulley to another attached to the near wheels. The body was in the form of a van and altogether a peculiar transport that seemed to work well enough. We had none or very little mail ourselves but occasionally the farmer did, so if we heard this vehicle approaching in the distance we would align ourselves in a position to get a lift to school and the driver being a kindly sort of chap we sometimes had this luxury.

Quite close to the school and on our route we had to pass an old railway carriage. How it had been transported there I don't know but it was the workshop of the local saddler. He didn't seem to object if we called in for a warm and the smell of leather was really wonderful. He was always well occupied and obviously very skilled as the horse in many forms was still very prominent in the early thirties. Another thing he did was to repair cricket balls for the surrounding village teams. He had a special holding device which enabled him to gradually turn the ball while he re-stitched the seam and then he would mallet it back into shape. I expect today a damaged ball would be thrown away but I can still see his gnarled hands doing an excellent job.

When eventually the elderly schoolmaster retired he was replaced by a headmistress called Mrs Cowey. She hailed from Northumberland and had this peculiar accent. She wasn't very popular with most of the local inhabitants but as it happened she proved a saviour to me.

I don't think our education had been badly neglected and we just went placidly along with what was on offer. We were rarely badly behaved I'm sure but I suppose most children just let their school life happen and wanted it to end so that they could get away and earn some sort of living. This was true of my brothers and sisters and they seemed happy enough with their lot. It is true to say that as kids we had no educational backing from home. For our parents it was all work and their lives revolved around a solid routine. We had no books to talk of in our lives at all and newspapers would have been a luxury that we could not afford. There was a gramophone which wound up and a few records and we had a radio which was quite good. It was powered by wet accumulator batteries that didn't last very long and one of our chores was to carry these batteries to the village store where there were charging facilities to get replacements. It was possible to get some foreign stations on the radio and I began to listen to some classical music from radio Luxembourg or radio Hilversham. This did not go down too well with the family and I was frequently told to switch that rubbish off. As a family we often used to hear commentaries on boxing matches which was something to look forward to. Our favourite heavyweights were Len Harvey, Joe Peterson and Jack London and we were very disappointed if they lost. This was also the era of some good foreign boxers such as Walter Neusel, Max Schmeling and Joe Louis so there were often some very exciting bouts.

Mrs Cowey was indeed a new broom at the school and looked the part with a severe bun and glasses. Two things that she introduced was an early morning session of mental arithmetic and a different approach to English. I suppose I must have somehow mastered my tables which seemed to be a must in those days. Her session started with her hurling rather difficult questions at the class (seniors) often to do with money. How many pence in a half crown? How many farthings in nine pence, how many sixpences in a guinea and many similar questions. These were interspersed with what is nine sevens? What are eleven eights etc. When a pupil answered five correctly they were allowed to stand at the back of the class. This became quite an honour and I think we really strived to achieve this. I suppose also it was her way of grading our ability.

Her method of teaching things English was to start the lesson with what was called 'dictation' in which she read a passage from a book and we listened and wrote it down. When this was marked it included the correction of spelling mistakes and once again we strived to do as well as possible. She marked our work from nought to ten and kept a record of our progress that was pinned on the wall.

This was usually followed by writing an essay from a list of subjects written on the blackboard. I can remember beginning to really enjoy school for the first time and was very disappointed if my essay mark was below seven out of ten.

For the first time in the school's history she decided to enter two pupils for the technical school at Cambridge. This was really a day trade school that offered building, engineering and painting to boys and needlework, domestic science and business training to girls. Some boy pupils did the business training course as well but generally speaking this was an exception. The two boys entered were farmer's sons and no doubt had a better educational background than we did and were considerably better off. Their names were Conrad Reeve and Kenneth Waller and they seemed to have passed the entrance exam with considerable ease. To get to Cambridge from Great Chishill was not easy and to travel the fourteen miles one had to cycle to Fowlmere and then get the school bus from there. The local inn keeper allowed pupils to put their cycles in an out building which was very considerate of him. The course at the technical school lasted two years and it was hoped that it would be an introduction to further education leading to a national certificate in the chosen subject.

This appointment was probably Mrs Cowey's first as a headmistress and her success with the two boys was as important to her as it was to the two pupils. She also must have known that to continue this success would not be easy as the raw material left would not have been very appealing. One of the boys namely Ken Waller had a sister who was a year younger than him and the same

16

age as I was. She became a candidate for possible further education and when I was also considered a very long chance I was pleased enough as well as being very apprehensive.

When approached about this my mother and stepfather were really taken aback as they knew it would lead to expense that they would have difficulty affording. Things like books, uniform and bicycles didn't come cheap and the prospect of providing such was a real worry. However Mrs Cowey pointed out that I would need to work exceptionally hard all round to achieve the required standard and bridges would have to be crossed when they were reached. So at the age of thirteen and very gauche I had to start to pull my socks up. I had an incentive that others didn't realise and I think in some ways it spurred me on. Joyce Waller was a very pretty young lady and considered to be the belle of the school and if we both succeeded in getting to the Tech we would be sort of thrown together. To me this was quite a prospect and when the elder boys left after their two years were up we would in fact have a whole year going to school by cycle and bus together.

Alas, things don't always turn out as planned! We both took the entrance examination and somehow I scraped through and she failed to pass. I always suspected that the Cambridge Education Authority allowed me to trickle through in deference to Mrs Cowey's obvious endeavours as I was certainly not at all sure that I had done well enough to pass. This was for me a real chance which I took to the best of my ability and during the two years in the building section I tried and succeeded in being around the middle or just above in the class.

There is a little bit of a sad note to all this. When Viv and I started at Great Chishill School at ten there was a girl in her last year at the school who would have been fourteen at the time who later married brother Gordon. After the Second World War, in fact many years after, I was visiting Gordon and his wife Freda and she said to me quite out of the blue, do you remember Joyce Waller who was at school with us? I of course said yes. Well, Freda said, she still lives at Great Chishill and when her farmer parents died she bought a cottage there. She never married and has lived a very reclusive life ever since. So I wonder now if the thought of being a pupil with me at the Technical School put her off trying at the exam. Perhaps not but it could have been so!

I think that some financial help was offered by the Cambridge Education Authority and as Viv would be leaving school and getting a job, things at home became better from the expense point of view. I at least was on my way to some further education and to this day I feel very grateful to the efforts of Mrs Cowey on my behalf.

At around this time Viv and I got second hand cycles which became very useful. They were bought at Royston market and were a bit small for us, having twenty inch diameter wheels but what a boon they were. I was invited to go on cycle rides at this time by Con Reeve who also owned an old cycle. His machine however, had a Sturmey Archer three speed gear arrangement and had twenty eight inch diameter wheels. I was rather small for my age at this time so my smaller cycle was not too incongruous but Con was almost six feet tall and a big strong lad. I think we must have looked an ill-assorted pair when we cycled together and I can remember having to pedal away very fast to keep up while he just went steadily along.

Farm life went on as usual and was very arduous work for male members of the family. This was especially so during the spring and summer months when the harvest had to be garnered. It was however a real farm insomuch as the land was set by ploughing (with horses) then harrowed and rolled and the seed planted. The crops were mainly cereals but things like mangel-wurzels and sugar beet were grown for feed for the animals, oats for the horses, corn for the chickens, beet for pigs etc. I worked on Saturday mornings and was paid the princely sum of ten shillings for about four hours work. I mainly helped the cowman who had the onerous job of milking by hand twice a day. He also used a machine that separated the cream from the skimmed milk and was altogether an important member of the farm. My main job was preparing feed and I can remember using a hand machine that sliced mangel-wurzels for pig food. It was exactly like the old kitchen mincing machines but much larger and you fed the beet into the top. By turning the handle which was quite hard work the revolving blades cut up the beet to manageable proportions.

During harvest time myself and other lads were employed to drive the tumbrel wagons from the corn fields to the corn stacks or harvester. The latter when used, would have been fed the corn sheaves from above and it threshed or sorted the corn from the straw. The corn ended up in sacks which weighed two hundredweights when full (224lbs) and these were taken usually to the barn for storage. The straw was also stacked and used as litter for all of the animals, and ended up as manure. This would eventually end up by being spread onto the fields as fertiliser for the next year's crops. Nothing was wasted. The threshing appliance was driven by a type of traction engine by a long belt and pulleys. The whole procedure was very messy and dusty, probably very unhealthy for the operators as well. This machine was however in great demand and was hired by all the local farmers so there was no hanging about once things had started.

Another job I really enjoyed was taking the horses to be shod by the village blacksmith. This meant riding on one horse and sometimes taking a second on a lead. The cart horses were very docile creatures and very easy to handle generally so this task was not too monumental. Sister Doreen was sometimes employed to take the riding hacks to the blacksmiths. She managed this quite well but I can remember mother being very annoyed when she returned home because she had a black imprint of the blacksmith's hand on her white stocking where he had given her a leg up on to the horse when about to return.

Having got our cycles my sister and I decided one Sunday to have an adventure. I cannot remember whose idea it was and thinking back on it I suppose it was a foolish thing to do! We had been to morning service as usual and in the afternoon instead of going to Sunday School we revolted! It was a lovely day weather-wise and we decided to visit sister Doreen at her hotel job in Newmarket which was twenty two miles away. There was little traffic on the road in those days especially on a Sunday and we made the journey on these small cycles without any problems.

Doreen, of course was flabbergasted to see us and we were invited into her room as she was off duty. I remember we had tea and sandwiches before being bundled back on our cycles as she realised we would have difficulty in getting back home before darkness settled. Meanwhile the hotel manager intervened and phoned the police at Royston to say where we were as by this time we should have been back home from Sunday School. Apparently the local constable informed our parents as to our whereabouts and said don't worry too much because if they made the journey one way they would be now well on the way back. Well it certainly caused a rare furore but make it back we did and quite an achievement in its way! I don't remember being badly censored for this escapade as I think there was an air of relief all round.

From a nourishment point of view we were well off during our five years or so on the farm. Eggs were no problem as we were allowed to have any misshapen or double ones so that Leslie always saw that we were well supplied in that department. We also had an adequate supply of skimmed milk as a perk so altogether we did well. Stepfather Perce kept the garden well stocked as was his wont so altogether we did quite well. In those days rabbits were considered a pest but at the same time part of our staple diet for meat. The two elder boys had permission to catch and sell the rabbits and ended up with quite a thriving little industry. They bought several ferrets and with nets and snares and the know-how they did very well. We had a travelling butcher who worked for Players the butchers in Royston and he delivered meat around the villages in a food van and he was always willing to take the rabbits off hand. My mother who had always been a country woman at heart taught the boys how to gut the rabbits and they soon became experts at it. There were often long rows of these creatures hanging up in the out house waiting for collection and often interspersed with the odd hare. Jugged hare was a delicacy in those days but the farmer did not encourage hare catching for the following reason.

On certain specific times of the year hare coursing events took place. Crowds would gather at these meetings and betting on the dogs was the object. The dogs were usually lurchers or whippets or sometimes greyhounds and a matched pair were released to chase and destroy the poor old hare who would have been put up in the middle of the field. The winning dog was the one who reached the hare first. Thinking back on this so called sport it seems an abominable practice but then, it was quite acceptable. Like fox-hunting it has now lost favour thank goodness!

About this time Mrs Cowey decided to introduce us kids to some drama of a sort. She selected passages from Longfellow's *Hiawatha* and we sang or acted these out. Some of the boys including myself became braves and we made tomahawks out of cardboard and sticks with headbands with chicken feathers in. We almost looked the part. The girls became squaws of course and the part of Minnehaha was prominent but I can't remember who played it. We had a chorus of braves who did some prancing but alas, my route to stardom was about to be demolished when we were lined up to sing some of the passages. Someone in this row is singing flat she said! And it didn't take her long to find out that it was me and so I was quickly demoted to stage management or something similar. I suppose she had a point as we were to put on a performance in the village hall and she didn't want it ruined. I tried to put this voice fact to some advantage on the following Sunday before the service began by telling the Vicar that I couldn't sing and didn't ought to be in the choir! He merely said that choirboys were hard to come by and I looked the part when in surplice and frock, whatever. I ended up as permanent organ blower which meant being in the back row of the choir and on hand to pump the organ when hymns were to be sung. Another plan that went awry!

Working things out my mother must have been born in 1886 because she died in 1968 at the age of 82. So at our time at Great Chishill she would have been in her mid forties. She therefore had been married to my stepfather for eight years when they produced a little daughter Pauline. I cannot think why they should have taken so long in deciding to start a family but they did!

Pauline was a pretty little girl and when a son Peter was born three years later things seemed to be going well enough. Sadly when she was four she died of meningitis and a few months later Peter died of the same malady. It was all so very sad and I remember being taken into the parlour to see Pauline in her small white coffin which is a memory that I will always carry in my mind as she looked so beautiful and peaceful. They were buried in the churchyard at Great Chishill in unmarked graves with just two lonely mounds along the church pathway to remind one that they ever existed.

When September 1935 came I was able and willing to start at the new school and really looking forward to it. My brother and twin sister appeared to be quite grumpy about this but I suspect this was to cover up their real feelings as they never in later life made an issue of my good fortune. I remember coming home after my first week and saying that I needed a technical drawing set and that it would cost ten and sixpence. This was quite a sum on top of everything else and didn't go down very well! It is strange to think that the set has survived for over seventy years and has been used for all my design work and I still use it today. The case is a bit battered but the contents are still functional. I made a pencil sharpener by gluing a piece of glass paper to a thin strip of wood and that also survives and is used.

I waited each school morning at the end of our land for the other two boys to arrive; they usually swept along at quite a speed so I had some difficulty in catching up. We realised after a few days that another lad was also on our route, he lived near the first crossroads and went to the Perse school in Cambridge. Perse meant posh and his uniform jacket was an amazing multi colour affair which made our blue jackets look very ordinary. There were several tiers of secondary education in Cambridge at the time. We were the lowest then the County school which catered for the more academic pupils, the Perse school came next and I suspect that most of the pupils would have been fee paying.

I got to know this boy quite well as we travelled together for the two years. His father worked in London and journeyed from Royston daily by train and they lived in a much higher tax bracket than we did. During those first few weeks we ribbed him unmercifully and considered him to be a sissy. We were not unkind and it was just friendly banter and he just laughed it all off. I am not sure that I could have coped the way he did and I still believe that I learned a lot about human nature from his stoicism. During our second year together I was asked round to tea on several occasions and I realised that they had an opulent lifestyle. His mother was quite a gracious lady but very welcoming. When he came to visit us we usually had tea and cakes outside in the garden as I must say I was a bit aware of our reduced circumstances.

That first year at the Tech seemed to go quite quickly! I cannot remember any bullying or unpleasantness among the pupils as I think we had a common purpose, to get on! Unfortunately the two practical teachers were of a bullying nature and as we spent half our week in the workshops, this created a problem that we had to tolerate. It is definitely true to say that they favoured some pupils more than others and that was fact! Perhaps I was not a particularly great personality at the time! Recently when looking through some old photographs I came across a snap of myself taken at about that time! Rather a thin loose limbed lad with glasses, hair parted centrally and a rather gormless look on my face and perhaps not very inspiring. Nevertheless we were all entitled to be treated equally at the start of the course and I certainly was not. The woodwork instructor had a very low opinion of me especially as I miserably failed to accomplish my first assignment. I had to make an oval mat from thin strips of wood, some were teak (brown) some were sycamore (white). These were about one inch wide by a quarter inch thick and nine inches long and my task was to plane the edges to fit. The pieces of wood were arranged alternately to get a pleasant pattern which if achieved would look very nice. The operative word here is *fit* and I spent week after week planing these edges and the pieces of wood got smaller and smaller and my self-esteem got lower and lower. Eventually after a considerable time he came to my bench with a look of disgust on his face and threw the dreaded pieces into the bin. We will start another job next week he said.

After sixty five years of being a craftsman, if those pieces of wood were handed to me today I would still have difficulty getting them to fit perfectly. The plane would need to be very sharp and finely set to take off cigarette paper thin shavings and handling the plane would require the greatest skill. That bloke was a moron really but it made me very determined to succeed in spite of his objectionable attitude and I think I did!

We spent one afternoon a week in the engineering department learning metalwork and I must say that I enjoyed the change. The instructor was a small man who didn't seem to have much patience but I learned things that were to be useful in later life. We made small tools, mainly some which required hardening and tempering and were useful for woodwork. I made a screwdriver bit that would fit into a carpenter's brace and an adjustable level that I used for many years.

The mathematics and science we did were geared to practical work and were enjoyable because they had real meaning! We learned about beam reactions, moments, fulcrums, forces and the maths related to a large extent to the work done by a quantity surveyor in building or a calculator of materials in engineering. We learned about the properties of material such as sand and cement and also how bricks were made and their density for certain purposes.

Welding material and solders were discussed and the work we did in the classroom was never boring. Our work was always done in exercise books so we could have recourse to our studies but we did not have homework set as such.

I remember very well the only outing we had during the course and it was by coach to the London Brick Company. They were situated strangely enough close to Bedford! It was a well organised trip and quite eye opening and enjoyed by our building section in particular. It was sad to hear recently that these works are gradually going into decline and will close probably in 2008. I suppose the advent of new materials such as large concrete sections and the technology in making huge slabs of glass have something to do with this.

From Fifteen to Twenty

This period of my life includes my second year at the technical school and the first year of my enforced army career.

We still lived at New Buildings for that first year, namely 1936 but it was to be our last year there as things were going to change.

Leslie had bought a second-hand Norton motorcycle and with it he was taking the monthly journal the 'Motor Cycle' which I found not only good reading but interesting. In fact it opened up a new world for both of us as there were articles on all facets of motorcycle life which included trials riding and racing. At that time the Norton and Velocette company machines were dominating the world racing circuits including the Isle of Man TT races, Manx Grand Prix and the Ulster Grand Prix and we followed all this with avid content.

It was at this time that Leslie left his chicken farm job and worked at a small garage which was sited at the Flint crossroad which was about three miles from where we lived. The Flint itself was a public house and this garage was opposite and the two together made the crossroads quite busy and at times quite dangerous. Leslie's new job was more as a petrol attendant than a mechanic but nevertheless he soon became a very proficient mechanic and spent the rest of his long life as one including five years in the R.E.M.E. which was his contribution to the Second World War. The man responsible for the garage had two jobs and on certain days of the week he was an AA patrol man with his yellow B.S.A. motorcycle and side car. Quite a common sight on the roads not only then but for many years after the war! Today the organisation works from vans and other more complicated retrieving vehicles but is still a flourishing business that includes insurance etc. Members of the AA displayed a prominent badge on their cars and it was the duty of the patrolmen mechanics to salute members when they passed them on the road. This would be considered a dangerous practice today with the heavy traffic and speeds that are common now. There were three petrol pumps at this garage, the most expensive being a brand called 'Euthol' at ls-7d a gallon, the next was the more familiar 'Shell' at ls-6d a gallon and the cheapest was 'Dominion' at ls-5d a gallon.

The AA man's name was Alec Pettit and he lived in a bungalow next to the garage with his wife and daughter. She was called Ruby and was quite an attractive young lady a year older than myself. In spite of this Leslie who at the time was eight years older than her used to take her off for rides on the pillion of his Norton. I think it was all fairly platonic but I can remember her mother not being very approving of the arrangement. Ruby and I used to eye one another with some interest at times but I never had a penny to spare so liaisons of any sort were out of the question.

The butcher boy who delivered our weekly joint end and colluded with my brother's rabbit trade was becoming more involved in our lives as he began to court my sister Doreen. They would eventually marry and in time had a son and daughter and their lives as they evolved became particularly entwined with mine. His name was Dennis Rogers and his home was in the town of Royston where he lived with his parents. He delivered our meat and to the farmer and other workers on Saturday evenings and you could almost set your watch to the time of his arrival which was about 5.30pm.

Viv and I had one treat a week which was a visit to the cinema in Royston and we really looked forward to this. It didn't matter what the film was, we just went as our night out but I can remember seeing Noel Coward's *Cavalcade* and other classics like *Sanders of the River* and many more. So we were able to exploit Doreen's romance with Dennis and cadge a lift to Royston in the butcher's van. This was very convenient but not always pleasant as the van ponged a bit and we just sat on the floor in the back on some sacking and thought ourselves very lucky. All very illegal of course and he used to let us off at the approach to town which meant a short walk but we were very grateful. To get home we travelled by service bus to Great Chishill from Royston and walked the two miles as usual to get home.

It was about this time that Leslie, did in my opinion, a very unusual thing. He sold his fairly ancient Norton and bought a Vincent HRD Comet Special on hire purchase terms. These machines were very special as they were hand built by the firm of H Davies at Stevenage in Hertfordshire. It was not a new model but was reputed to have lapped the Brooklands racing circuit at a 100 plus miles per hour. I have no doubt that this was true as Leslie took me on the pillion to Newmarket by way of the six mile Bottom road and he reached a speed of 100 MPH for a short period. This stretch of road is now bypassed on the main route to Ipswich and the Suffolk coast but still exists as a very straight six mile stretch of secondary road. Quite something in those days but it is true to say that motor vehicles as well as motorcycles were being built for speed and reliability and achieving phenomenal results on various race tracks and circuits all over Europe as seen by the TT results of the time.

When Leslie and Gordon were conscripted for war service in 1938 Leslie still owed a considerable sum on the HRD motorcycle and he lost a lot of money when he had to return it to the farm. His son who lives in Belfast has a fairly large of portrait of his father seated on the HRD and looking young and handsome in a smart leather jacket and I guess I will always remember him in that way!

The Flint garage where Leslie worked was at a midway point between London and Newmarket and during the flat racing season the route was exceptionally busy. Bookmakers, punters and other people associated with horse racing turned the road from a quiet one to a maelstrom of fast moving horse vans, cars, bookies, Rolls Royces and many other forms of traffic. The garage did a roaring trade and both Leslie and Alec Pettit were very fully occupied. The winners on the return journey were very generous and I think the workers had a field day. I remember Leslie gained quite a few gallons of petrol as some of the motorists paid for more than the vehicles could hold and of course the pumps were hand operated which could also add to the fiddle. He certainly ran his bike very economically but at the same time it was very hard work.

My second year at the technical school was fairly uneventful. We worked hard still and the teachers were in the main very efficient and demanded good results. We seemed to have more time for leisure and played cricket and football against other schools as well as interschool events. These all took place on Parker's Piece which was a very large type of park quite near the school. During lunch breaks we often took our sandwiches to the far side of the park and by climbing up to the top of a fairly high wall we could see the Varsity cricket team play the various counties during the season.

In those days the University team always played Worcester in their opening match and we looked forward to these events. No one seemed to mind us doing this and I can't remember being told off although I suppose it was quite illegal. These were happy days and not too stressful and I suppose my two years of secondary education were a very good grounding for the years to follow.

We were coming to the end of our own stay at the farm and those years were very pleasant also! Our general food requisites and in fact many essential items were delivered to the door. Groceries came by CWS van once a week. The Cooperative Wholesale Society were big business at the time and that is where the food that we didn't grow came from. I remember enjoying their pork pies which were quite large and crusty, the meat had a jelly on top and the whole pie was very tasty. Viv and I used to halve one and they were nice. Our butchers of course was well organised and we had a traveller who came from Bishop's Stortford who brought clothes and curtain samples and the like to the door. Mum had some sort of monthly payment scheme with him and details of monies were kept in a notebook.

The insurance man was also a regular visitor. I don't know any details of this but things like penny policies were quite common. I remember him well because he came by motorcycle and sidecar, the latter being bullet shaped and streamlined and pulled by a Triumph bike. Another weekly visitor was the oil man and his van took the form of a utility shop rather like an open all hours shop on wheels. He passed by the end of the lane quite late on Friday evenings and we had to meet him with our oil containers and shopping bags. Our main lighting was by oil lamp or by candles when going to bed and he had both. Anything you bought from him seemed to be impregnated with paraffin oil but he still seemed to do a good trade. Viv and I were allowed a penny or tuppence to spend on sweets and boiled ones were by far the cheapest but we enjoyed these oil impregnated sweets all the same and thought ourselves lucky to get them.

Quite a common sight at the time and an unusual one was door to door salesmen that were of Indian origin. The men in full Indian costume complete with turban used to carry large suitcases of clothes and hawk them round the countryside. They seemed to be very polite and not at all pushy and their wares varied from ordinary haberdashery to exotic silks. This must seem strange today but then this was quite common, some of them walked prodigious distances but others had cycles that they pushed with the cases attached to the cycle. They seemed to make some sort of living and must have had some sort of centre perhaps in small towns.

A few weeks before the end of my last term at school we had interviews for suitable work. It seemed that prospective employers liaised with the Education Authority and this careers man arrived with a list of vacancies. I was offered a choice of two jobs and more or less told that I would be wise to accept one of them. They were both apprenticeships: one was with Pye radio and the other with a buildings firm as a joiner. I went on my own to the radio firm. They were a big concern and leaders at their time in that field and their wares well advertised. It was a kindly man who I saw at the interview and he asked a few pertinent questions which I coped with quite well I thought. Then he said, what metal is used at the heated end of a soldering iron and to my shame I did not know. This didn't say much for my metalwork teaching but to my surprise at the end of the appraisal he said that he thought a technical school pupil could be an asset to the firm and I was offered a job! On the way to his office I had had to walk through the assembly building which was very large and housed row upon row of lighted benches. Each work person seemed to be soldering components together and fixing them to a metal base or chassis. To me even at my tender inexperienced age it seemed rather a soul destroying job. I explained to the man that I did have another interview and he pointed out the job offered good prospects and he mentioned cabinet design and other facets of the industry. He also said that all new workers did a spell on the assembly lines, this was normal procedure which was rather off putting.

For the building apprenticeship interview I had to be accompanied by a parent so Mother and I duly turned up at the main offices of Caulson & Son Builders in the centre of Cambridge. The lady we saw was middle aged, quite grey and wore glasses and her position with the firm was the one of 'secretary'. Her name was Miss Schoot and she was obviously of East European extraction and during the next few years at the firm I came to realise how important a cog she was in the running of the firm, in that it almost revolved around her. She explained the terms of the apprenticeship regarding duration and pay and also legal aspects which would be binding on both parties. She also said that if I continued my studies at the further education part of the technical school and eventually passed the National Building Certificate I would be considered for advancement in the firm. This meant that if I did two evening classes, I could have Saturday mornings off work to attend this further education. This seemed to be very good and she mentioned that if I got the Certificate I could progress from being a joiner to further training towards being a certified quantity surveyor. Well, we decided to sign the necessary indenture forms and I became an employee for the first time in my life. My wages for the first year would be one sixth of a man's wages and this turned out to be 8s 4d or one hundred pence in old money. During my second year it would be one fifth and then one quarter during the third year and that was how it was worked out. Pretty poor pay really but the training was good. I was put to work with a very good joiner and we shared a bench in a large airy workshop filled with a long row of similar benches. This was like an assembly shop but the work was very varied, one day we might be making casement window frames, the next kitchen fitments etc.

During my second year the firm was involved with contract work for the new Sidney Sussex College. This was a new red brick building and we had the privilege of making the staircases, panelling and some furniture such as wardrobes and other fitments. We used top quality Japanese oak for this and the work had to be of the highest standard. This was where my joiner partner came really into his own and I learned a great deal about not only skill but pride in one's work. His name was Billy Reed and he was one of the firm's longest serving retainers. I can remember the other apprentices (and there were about 8 of varying ages) betting me that I couldn't ever get a date with his daughter. She *apparently* was quite a comely young lady and he was *apparently* very protective of her thinking that these young lads were not for her. It seemed that all these lads had at some time tried to get him to invite them to Sunday tea in order to make her acquaintance but without success and so they opened the challenge to me. Well! It is true to say that I was also unsuccessful but with my wages and prospects I really didn't try too hard.

Just before we finally left the farm at Great Chishill I got to know quite well the vicar's son. He was at the village school for a short time before I left there but in his position as a choir member and bell ringer we mixed quite a lot. His name was Donald Kingaby and he did his further education at the Cathedral Church School at Ely in Cambridgeshire. I was pleased to have known him as he became a leading and very successful fighter pilot in World War Two and distinguished himself in the Battle of Britain. He features in many books written about that era and I recently read a book called *The Darlington Spitfire* in which he played a prominent part. He survived the war and retired as a Squadron Leader. He died in America where he went to live with his daughters and he was a very brave man but somehow it is a bit strange to think of his father as a village parson.

It was also at about this time that Leslie's friend at the garage was killed. At the Flint crossroads between one of the intersections stood the AA cabin in which he conducted his AA business. And while he was in there one day a fast travelling car lost control and demolished the cabin with him in it. I can't remember being told any details but it was a terrible tragedy for his wife and daughter. I remember that Leslie was put in charge of the garage and remained employed there until his eventual army call up late in 1938. Alec's wife had to leave the bungalow and both she and Ruby the daughter moved to the small town of Sawston near Cambridge and got jobs at the large paper mill works that was situated there.

Quite suddenly and entirely out of the blue we were once again on the move and what a change of circumstances it was! My mother saw an advertisement in the local Royston paper by the War Office or some similar department asking for married couples to take over furnished accommodation for men working on the hangers at runways at Bassingbourn aerodrome. It was on a temporary basis of about two years and the large house would accommodate about twelve workers. The money for doing this must have been quite substantial and my mother I'm sure realised that it would be extremely hard work. How she persuaded step father Perce to leave the farm I don't know but I think they saw an opportunity to make some quick cash and they took it.

The house itself was three storied and was fully furnished to take these workers with sufficient bed space for them and a large kitchen and dining room. Our home was the top storey which was like a row of attics and was quite comfortable. My mother's commitment was to feed these men and their bedding was also her responsibility. If she did their washing (no machines in those days) they had to pay her individually for that. The aerodrome was being constructed for large bombers and was actually at Kneesworth which was really an extension of Bassingbourn so the workers had to travel almost a mile to get to work, some walked and some cycled. The men were quite a mixed bunch and their jobs varied from concrete workers to steel construction assemblers.

We got to know them quite well during those two years and there was some coming and going as the project advanced. This to me was quite an educational experience as they came from various parts of the country. With war approaching this was a rush job and the base played quite a big part during the dire struggle that ensued between 1939-1945.

During the first two years of my working at Caulsons the builders I had full time problems of my own. The move to Bassingbourn meant that I was faced with a twelve mile journey to get there. I was provided with a full sized bike that had a three speed gear box and was semi sporty with handlebars that when reversed lowered the riding position: great when combating the head winds that were surely to come. So, my task was to cycle twelve miles to Cambridge to start work at 8am then work until 5pm and cycle home. On Tuesdays and Wednesdays the task was rather more difficult as I was required to stay in Cambridge to do evening classes. These started at 7.15pm and finished at 9.15pm and with the winter of 1938 approaching this added problems indeed. Cycle lighting at the time was very primitive and was only useful to show other travellers where you were on the road and not very good at illuminating one's road ahead. There was no option but to cope with these problems as they arose but as the winter passed my mother did become aware of them and to my delight she forked up six pounds and suggested that with Leslie's acumen to help we could try the market for a second hand motorcycle. During the next three and a half years I had four rather decrepit machines to cope with and there were times when I seemed to do more pushing than riding. This was, however, a large learning curve in my life as I had to become a maker, mender and general mechanic in order to keep going. As well as adding a useful skill to my life it was also very character building and with my brother's help and undoubted mechanical knowledge I benefited considerably and became quite self-sufficient. I must add that the occasional illicit gallon of petrol from his garage also paved the way to my smooth motorcycling.

In 1938 brother Gordon married Freda and they also lived in Bassingbourn! They were not happily accommodated as they had two rooms in a local pub and with a child on the way this was not ideal! To make matters worse he got notice of his impending call up to the army. He had had previous notice of this and had applied to join the RHA (Royal Horse Artillery) being an agricultural worker, this seemed sensible. Things did not work out quite as expected and he was in for rather a surprise. He had to report for his military training to quite a nice sounding rural HQ in Dorset but as things transpired it also turned out to be the HQ for one of the largest tank training units in Britain. The cavalry units of the army were being rapidly mechanised and before too long he was travelling around the moors in a large tank. Still he adapted well and was promoted to a tank commander. He served throughout the African desert campaigns and followed that with a stint in Italy. During this time he was wounded by blast and although he got some home leave he was back in action after a few weeks. He was very proud of his war service and had a string of medals for his brave efforts.

He returned to agricultural activities after the war working as a gang leader of a team that picked and produced vegetables. This meant working in appalling conditions at the crack of dawn to get produce to Covent Garden Market each day. That was how he spent the rest of his working life and he and Freda lived in council accommodation. They had a daughter by this time and today she lives at Melbourne near Royston, not far from that notorious Flint cross roads. Gordon suffered to some extent from his war activities and the nature of his work and had both hips replaced during later life. I suppose you would describe him in modern parlance as a tough cookie and he was! I remember at his funeral that Freda said she had pinned his medals on his chest in his coffin and she preferred for him to be buried rather than cremated. That was their country way and he was interred in the extended burial ground at Bassingbourn.

The work on Bassingbourn aerodrome was nearing completion and my parents were once again on the move. Perce never had problems with getting suitable farm work and this time our destination was a farm in the village of Littlebury Green which was about eleven miles from Cambridge and five from the pretty town of Saffron Walden, Essex.

We had a small house in the village centre near the local pub and I have no recollection of the farm itself as none of us except step father was involved. The town of Saffron Walden was very pleasant to visit and the road there from our direction passed the large country estate of Audley End and the house and parkland could be seen from the road. The town itself had useful facilities including a cinema and various parks etc and we had many enjoyable visits there.

Work and travel went on as usual for me. I still had the problems with unreliable motorcycles and had occasional break downs when pushing the bike home during unpleasant foggy weather after a late evening class which was a memory not to be enjoyed. The war by now had started and the quality of work tended to get poor. I can remember being sent to a large house in Hertfordshire called Lower Hare Park to take measurements to black out all the windows as it was to become an army HQ of some description. This was quite a responsible job as the black out frames were to be made in the workshop and then transported back and fitted. This meant some structural damage to the heavy mullioned windows but it had to be done.

Cambridge itself was beginning to suffer from air raids and the station seemed to be a target for returning bombers to jettison their loads if they had been prematurely turned back. On several occasions we saw the bombs falling on the station which was about a mile away from our work place. Casualties were quite high and pedestrians in the area were killed by blast.

In 1939 Leslie received his calling up papers and like Gordon had been given some choice in his deployment. Being mechanically minded he joined the REME (Royal Electrical and Mechanical Engineers) and for some obscure reason was sent to Belfast and did his training there!

Before the war he was a carefree kind of person, rather naughty at times and not adverse to doing a bit of poaching or petrol fiddling and the like! This was about to change as in Ireland he met a devout protestant girl and was soon married.

She and her family had a big influence on his whole life from then on and he seemed to become really engrossed in religion. Nevertheless they had a good life together and had two children, a girl 'Jean' and later after the war a son 'Eric'.

After a short spell in Ireland he was drafted overseas to India and Burma and was soon promoted to a Sergeant Instructor and he spent most of his war on the Burmese border training Indian soldiers on maintaining and servicing Daimler scout cars. This particular vehicle had fluid flywheel transmission which was quite an advance on clutch type traction and he had had to go on a special course to get the necessary training. After his war he returned to Belfast and worked for the electricity board as a heavy crane driver. His main job seemed to be transporting heavy transformers to various outlandish places in Ireland.

He always retained his enthusiasm for motor cycles and although they had a family car he also kept a bike for his personal use. When he was seventy he had quite a serious accident on the bike in the heavy traffic in Belfast and this resulted in the loss of a leg just above the knee. His latter years alas, were not very comfortable and he suffered a great deal. He managed to keep mobile by driving an automatic car and with his indomitable spirit they still managed to get quite a lot out of life. He used to phone me about once a month as we always kept in contact and he and Anne (his wife) would go on trips in the car along the coast. They had a favourite place to visit and from there they could see Scotland on a clear day. I often thought he sounded a bit homesick when he said that. Another topic on the phone was religion and he did his best without much success to convert me. Not that I have anything against religion and if people get comfort from their beliefs that to me is fine. I think my enforced forays into church and choir as a child had turned me in a different direction. Anne was slightly older than Leslie and in her late seventies developed Alzheimer's disease and she became quite a big worry to her family before she was institutionalised and eventually died. This was a big blow to Leslie as they were a very devoted couple and he no doubt felt difficulty in coping. He was approaching ninety years of age when he died and his latter years were anything but pleasant for him. Rather a sad ending but overall he packed quite a lot into his life with his many interests.

During my eighteenth year the type of work available at the building firm was very mundane. For a short period in 1939 myself and the other apprentices were reduced to making camouflage nets for the services. The netting was laid out on a large open space and strips of fawn or green webbing had to be inserted in and out of the mesh. We turned this process into a game in which we raced each other from one side of the large net to the other. This also got the boring job done more quickly which pleased everybody! I had become quite friendly with another apprentice by this time and his name was Ron O'Dell. We were the same age and had similar status with the firm but he was favoured to some extent as his father had worked with Caulsons for many years in the decorating side of the business. I often allowed him to ride my motorcycle on the quiet roads of Cambridgeshire and he became quite proficient and this was to turn out in his favour as will be seen later on in this narrative. He was a very keen coarse fisherman and he introduced me to the sport and this worked out very well as we frequently went on fishing trips to the local rivers such as the Ouse and Bedford. He provided the fishing equipment and I the transport and we spent many hours on the river sides with great enjoyment. Having almost perfect eyesight he was very good at the sport and was able to see his float even when the water was choppy. I struggled in this department but on one occasion I did catch a 2.5lb bream which became the height of my success and never to be forgotten. There was a stretch on the old Bedford river that was tidal to some degree and we often caught flat fish such as dabs. We used bugworm as bait and tended to trawl the river bed which worked very well.

Ron and I both had notice of call up at about the same time as we were approaching our nineteenth birthdays in 1940. It was at this time the second deciding event in my life took place that was to shape things for me and Ron for the next five and a half years.

One of the regular joiners at the firm was a keen motorcyclist and owned a beautiful HRD black shadow bike. This was a 1000cc twin machine with a spring frame and many other de luxe features and was in fact the flag ship of the HRD range. The man's name was Francis Ffoulkes and he was rather an eccentric character. He seemed old to us but was probably in his mid thirties, he was a confirmed bachelor and lodged with an elderly lady who tended to mother him and allowed him to keep his spotless motorcycle in her scullery. We could never understand how he missed the draft and when we queried this he mumbled something about flat feet or reserved occupation but I am sure the latter didn't apply.

One lunch time when he was reading his monthly copy of the 'Motorcycle' he called me over to where he was sitting and said 'young Nixon, this might interest you'. He showed me a full size page WD advertisement. This stated that the Royal Corps of Signals required despatch riders and that volunteers with riding experience, subject to passing a medical examination were needed to replace losses in France and Dunkirk. The icing on the cake was that formal training such as drilling would be forgone and the specialised training for the job would be carried out when you joined the trained unit.

This all sounded great to us and after conferring with Ron we decided to fill in the application form forthwith.

While awaiting a reply from the War Office Ron and I did our last pre-war job for Caulsons. We were sent to the Fitzwilliam museum to measure and fit protective shields to prevent blast damage from blowing in the windows and damaging the fixed exhibits. The windows were large and probably fifteen feet high by about eight feet wide and we were to make these up using thick blockwood. These heavyweight shutters had to be strengthened and buttressed into place and strutted to heavy blocks screwed to the floor. The job was successfully completed and a chapter of our lives ended.

A few days later we had a letter and railway warrant telling us to report to an address near Liverpool Street Station for interviews and medical examination. This being completed we were at once waiting for developments. I was a bit worried about the medical because of my eyesight but within a few days we were sent details of our unit and were on our way to Sussex to join 4 Corps signals.

We eventually arrived at these headquarters at about 4 o'clock on a Friday and were met at the station and transported back to the orderly room where we were met by a kindly seeming sergeant. He showed us to our sleeping quarters and said we would not be processed until Monday morning and would then report to the main hall at 10 o'clock, meanwhile we were advised to make the most of the weekend. He mentioned some of the delights of the local town which was East Grinstead. This all sounded very civilised and I thought that perhaps the dear old country was not so hard up for us soldiers after all.

On the Monday when entering the hall we were surprised to find about one hundred other volunteers and on the stage were several officers and senior NCOs and we were to be addressed by the training officer who was a major. After a welcoming speech he said that 4th Corp needed personnel in all the main signalling trades, particularly as tele-printer and despatch riders. He emphasised that many of us volunteers were ex post office workers and should fit into the scheme of things very well. He went on to paint the importance and relevance of the various trades and that at this stage if anyone wanted to change from their chosen trade they could do so. After this we were divided into groups and Ron and I found ourselves with ten other intended despatch riders under the supervision of two sergeants! It turned out that they had been despatch riders themselves but had decided to change trades. We queried this as they seemed to be very amicable blokes and they said that promotion as DR was not possible and since they had both married soon after the Dunkirk fiasco they needed the extra money that came with advancement.

The training course itself was very interesting but came as quite a shock to all of us. Riding a motor cycle was taken for granted and had we thought it was a question of just riding and away we were to be disappointed. Most of the first week of the six week course was on machine maintenance and we found ourselves given engine or frame parts to assemble. We were expected to repair a puncture and refit the tube and tyre to a wheel in a set time! We were also given due warnings about keeping our machines in top condition at all times and of the consequences if we failed to do this. On the Thursday of that first week we were issued with a riding kit and also a 500cc side valve Norton machine, model 16H and were told to prepare the machine for an excursion on the next day. This was more like it! And away we went next morning in convoy with one

NCO at the front and the other at the rear. At last we were mobile and after a few miles of road work we entered into the hard part as we left the road and found ourselves following a trial route. This was mainly along a shallow stream with sandy boulders and other hazards and occasionally a bit of hill climbing. These machines weighed about 3cwt, far heavier than any bike I had ever ridden and returning to base I was aware that my abilities as a motorcyclist had been severely tested. I guessed that in the pecking order of the twelve of us the sergeants would be rating me at about tenth from the top. Physical strength definitely played a part in all this but I consoled myself with thinking that I could compete well enough on the road where hopefully we would be doing most of our DR work. In truth the NCOs didn't say much but we were sure that they had some sort of ongoing report going.

That Friday evening we were given another shock and were handed out two pieces of printed paper. The information on one consisted of about ninety initials of army, navy and airforce units which had to be learned and we would be tested on a set number of them near the end of the course. Some were quite easy such as M.U meaning maintenance unit, A.O.C meaning air officer commanding, C.N.O meaning chief naval officer and so on. We had about five weeks to learn these in our spare time so it was not too bad.

On the second piece of paper was printed the Morse code which we also had to learn and were told that we would be going to the radio school for the next week and would learn to send and receive messages by Morse code. We would be expected to be able to send out fifteen words per minute and receive at ten words per minute by the end of that week.

I found this sudden academic work relatively easy as I had been studying at the building firm for those intervening years and I suppose I had a fresh mind for the work. Some of the other trainees found this side of the work hard going and I felt that I had recovered some ground lost perhaps in the riding part of the course.

The third week of the course was a mixture as it included map and compass reading. The maps were first class ordnance survey ones and we had to study the features of the maps in the class room before we were given the coordinates that would take us to set destinations. This part was really very interesting and I think we all enjoyed this aspect of the work. We were taught to use the compass but its use did not figure much in the rest of the training.

It seemed to the signals policy that various trades overlapped as we spent the fourth week learning elementary cable laying and jointing and a spell as a telephone operator, we were told that eventually we would be taught to drive vehicles up to three tons as well. I suppose this made sense as it meant that we had knowledge to repair telephone lines, familiarity with field telephones and generally knew how to cope with emergencies.

The final tests were to take place during the sixth and last week and the fifth week was a revision week. It unfortunately produced a nasty incident in which I was involved. We were all told that on a certain day we would accompany a trained despatch rider on an actual D.R. run. This meant watching how the despatches were docketed and signed for and delivered to the various units on the scheduled run. This could be likened to a postal delivery as we know it but done at high speed to a set timetable. So we set off that morning all going in different directions to the timetabled HQs in spread out East Sussex. There could be no hanging about and following another rider at a quick speed was not easy. My man and I were about half way through our round when rounding a fairly sharp bend we saw that there had been an accident. Another pair had been negotiating the same bend from the opposite direction and the following rider had run out of road and hit a tree stump on his right hand side of the road. The two qualified despatch riders soon decided what to do and said they must continue their rounds and my man said that he would report what had happened at his next call and see that an ambulance would be on its way to the scene as soon as possible and off they went. This gave me the chance to examine my poor colleague who was laying on his back at the roadside. It was easy to see that he was in great pain as his shin bone had been shattered when hitting the tree stump and blood and bone could be seen through his trouser leg. He seemed to be drifting in and out of consciousness and a sorry sight but I could do nothing to help. In fact I decided to examine his machine and was doing some first aid repairs to it when after what seemed hours the army ambulance arrived.

The M.O. (medical officer) was a captain and accompanied by a corporal was soon cutting away at the poor man's trousers to reveal the real damage. I remember him asking how long it had been since the accident but I could only give him an approximate figure of time. He decided that he would have to set the leg immediately and explained the procedure as the corporal began preparations. I was apparently to be part of all of this and was not too sure how I would react but it seemed that I was to begin being a real soldier on that day.

By this time the corporal had produced a circular metal frame that was put over the leg and a strap attached to it was handed to me to put over the man's shoulder and fix to the other side of the frame. A cord was attached to the man's ankle in such a way as by twisting the rope the leg could be pulled straight gradually so that the M.O. could push the splinters of the wound back in place. This of course was taking place at the opposite end to where I was holding the shoulder strap. This all seemed to go well and obviously the morphine injection given at the start of proceedings had done the job. When satisfied the medical men bandaged the area and applied splints and a difficult job had been completed.

The M.O. said that my fellow trainee would be unlikely to ride motor cycles again but at least his leg had been saved. This was certainly part of a learning curve for me and an insight to the sort of thing that could happen. The medical team for their part seemed very proficient and it was good in a way to be part of a team.

By this time a lorry from our HQ had arrived to transport the damaged bike to the repair shop and I merely had to find my way back and report my part of the proceedings to the CSM . Episode over.

Our final week of training turned out to be more of an assessment than actual set tests and thinking back I guess that the army signals needed replacement tradesman too much to fail the candidates! It was a fact that several of our group did not do well at the more academic side of the course but perhaps they made up for that in the more practical aspects. When the results went up on the daily orders board this included all the trades; there had been some overall failures and these were to become assistant cooks or general duties staff, still in fact an essential asset to the corps overall.

I felt a bit smug at this point as I had got DRII rating whereas the others were all DRIII, this merely meant a few pence extra a day but it looked nice in my AB64 which was the army paybook. Together with that fact I had been classified AI medically and blood group A2 (not common old O) I felt quite happy about things, but not for long as it turned out.

Our training sergeants seemed reasonably happy with us as a bunch. On a sunny Monday in early July we were officially handed our side arms (Smith and Wesson 38 revolvers) and our permanent motor cycles and given our survey maps and in addition, a co-ordinate map reference! We were told to be there and on arrival we found the place was a lovely old Sussex pub and as we arrived we received a great pint of bitter paid for in advance by our tutors. Our estimation of NCOs rocketed quite a bit that day and life didn't seem bad at all.

For me however, things were about to take a down turn. It must be said that general hygiene did not fit into the army's scheme of things particularly regarding food. The area behind the coalhouse was a horrible smelly mess with wasps, flies and other insects in abundance. It seemed that all the waste food collected for about a week at a time and then a farm vehicle would arrive to collect it all for the pig swill.

There had been a few reported cases of diphtheria in the area but as usual one never expects things like that to happen to oneself.

A few nights later I woke at some early hour with a terrible sore throat. We were sleeping in a large barn on straw palliases at the time and I remember dragging myself over many recumbent bodies to reach the barn door where I knew there was a cold water tap and large sink.

The next thing I knew I was waking up or regaining consciousness some forty eight or so hours later in East Grinstead isolation hospital.

When able to comprehend, ward sister told me that apparently I had had a lucky escape. It seemed that I had collapsed in the barn doorway and that one of the soldiers on guard duty while on his way to the toilet had spotted me in the doorway and reported it to the duty NCO. They must have acted very quickly to get me to the hospital and the ward sister said that had I not received prompt attention my throat would have closed causing death.

To this day I never found out who my guard benefactor was as I was destined not to return to my unit.

I began to realise how serious it could have been a few days later. It appeared that the patient in the bed next to me at the end of the ward had had to have a tracheotomy to save his life. I of course didn't know what this meant at the time and I was just glad to be seen to be making progress.

On each side of the ward was a row of beds, most of them occupied by soldiers in various stages of recovery. They delighted in telling me that I had been getting preferential treatment to their neglect from nurse Paris, who at the time I did not know existed. I queried this with the ward sister who told me that nurse Paris was a young practitioner and she had been very concerned about me during the previous few days. Apparently the nurse in question was off duty at that time. As it transpired we did form a liaison both being young and naive and during my convalescence period went for a few outings to cinemas and walks etc. Of course I knew and expect she did as well that I would be off and away soon because war time was like that!

After about a week in the end bed I was moved to a side bed which meant being slightly nearer the exit at the far end. There was a set procedure to follow and I was to begin it! Each day a throat swab was taken early in the morning and in order to be clear of the diphtheria infection you had to have three negative results that were consecutive. This could take several weeks to achieve as often two negative swabs could be followed by a positive one. I got the impression that some of the older soldiers in there were happy to prolong this procedure as they were being well fed with soft beds and almost home from home.

The young soldier who had had the throat operation was only making slow progress. He was able to breathe normally again but it seemed that he was a carrier of the infection and was told that it could be a very long time before he could expect to get negative results.

From entering the hospital to being cleared of infection plus an enforced convalescence took nearly eight weeks. This was bad news as it meant being 'Y' listed and a non return to your previous unit. This was normal army procedure and was to do with keeping units up to strength and ready for overseas duty.

I was summoned one day to matron's office and given details of my immediate future. She had a railway warrant for me and clearance papers and I would be departing in two days to the signals holding battalion at Kirkburton near Huddersfield. This was not good news as I had visions of being involved in foot slogging and back to basic military training. When I arrived I found the place relatively quiet and was told by the orderly sergeant that reposting to another unit would not take too long, however he informed me that I had an interview next day with the C.O. who it appeared was a Lt. Colonel.

This seemed strange as I was not aware of being in any trouble or doing anything contrary to military procedures but didn't worry too much as tomorrow was not too far away.

Next day I reported as required and was told to wait as the C.O. was dealing with a defaulters parade. It seemed that some of the recruits had been drinking or something similar and were being awarded various terms of C.B. (confined to barracks) for their misdemeanours.

My turn came and he seemed a reasonable sort of chap but not in the best of moods and I was not about to improve things for him. It seemed that with my papers that had come from my previous unit, the training officer had recommended me for further training as an instructor. The C.O. pointed out that the army was all about fitting round pegs in round holes and that although being a despatch rider was good there was not too much room for advancement and that I would be well advised to think seriously about the offered course.

At nineteen years of age and just having completed an arduous course of training I respectfully disagreed saying that I had not proved myself in that trade and did not want to do further training.

He pointed out again that the offer was a golden opportunity for me and that I could be a sergeant instructor in six months and that could lead to a commission. I still dug my heels in and he gave me a day to think it all over but in truth I did not feel that with my limited experience I was ready for all this.

A few days later my name appeared on the notice board, that I was posted to 27 AIR FORMATION SIGNALS UNIT which was being formed at Colwyn Bay in North Wales.

The new unit was to be a self-contained one of about fifty personnel of all the signal trades. When fully formed it would be attached to an RAF wing and would be responsible for its communications.

The man in charge was young 2nd lieutenant not much older than I was. He seemed to be very keen and had probably been to University and a good school and seemed a nice enough man. There were two sergeants who were both post office trained one being a technical type and the other administrative and they were both very efficient. When I arrived the unit was far from complete and for the next few months various people were acquired to make up the full complement. This eventually took about six months but in that time all the relevant equipment and vehicles had arrived so we were almost ready to go.

Our time in Colwyn Bay was very pleasant and our evenings were free. I remember at the time there was a scenic trolley bus service that went along the coast and it was an enjoyable ride. We used it frequently as it was a cheap ride and we often ended at the Great Ormes head at Llandudno, having a good pint. Much of our day time was spent in the usual army way beginning with early morning PT which comprised of a quick sprint to the pier and physical jerks in the pavilion. We did route marches as well and we thought ourselves quite impressive strutting through the town. We were kept on our toes by study despatch procedures and even had to keep our Morse speech up to scratch, and were kept fully occupied.

Three of my DR colleagues were Scottish, the two other English ones turned out to be quite experienced but as all five had DRIII ratings I found myself nominally in charge as my DRII rating said so! In fact this hardly mattered as by nature a DR, once he had left the signal office became his own master and only he could be responsible for the despatches he carried. Two of the Scottish lads were about my age and both were a bit wild and at times even reckless. On pay days they tended to live it up with drink and gambling and were in hot water on several occasions. For most of the time they were sensible enough and intelligent and eventually learned the hard way by getting their liberty curtailed with CB. I became quite friendly with the other Scot and we often went out together in the evenings. He was a dour type and married so he had little money left for frivolities after his wife's allowance was deducted from his wages. It was army policy to get the soldiers even if single to have part of their earnings deducted and sent home. My mother collected this for me for the whole five years plus that I was in the army but it still did not amount to a large sum. I spent mine in acquiring a second hand motorcycle after I was demobbed and the whole amount would not have been more than fifty pounds.

From Twenty to Twenty-Five

I had my twentieth birthday just before we left Colwyn Bay. During the six months or so we were there we had lived in private houses that were empty and seconded by the forces. As we were destined to become an integral part of an RAF wing we had no domestic people in the unit and relied on food, laundry and other services to be supplied. For our food in Colwyn Bay we had merely taken our knife, fork and spoon and mess tin to another local unit that had fed us and that was how it was.

We had known from the beginning that the unit was destined to go overseas and as Colwyn Bay is not too many miles from Liverpool we imagined that we would get some leave eventually and go from that port. Those in command had other ideas and on some date late in May 1941 we found ourselves as a small convoy heading for RAF Hendon. The weather was absolutely foul with continuous rain all day. The waterproof capes issued to despatch riders were reasonably good but the leggings were similar to those worn by cyclists of the time and came from the ankle to the crotch only, which meant that rain cascading down onto the motorcycle penetrated the seat area leading to much discomfort. Well, it was a reasonably warm May and we just had to endure it all. We had two riders at the front leading the route, followed by the officer in a fifteen hundred weight truck preceding the two heavier three ton trucks. The first one had the operators and the teleprinters with the wireless sets and the instrument mechanic! The third truck must have looked a bit peculiar with several telephone poles sticking out of the front at an angle and it also conveyed the linesmen and several types of cable drums. The four DRs at the rear were often relayed to the front as the leading DRs were stopping at various junctions to make sure that no vehicle took a wrong turning. Having got to Hendon we concluded that it had been some sort of practice run but at least it had gone fairly smoothly.

Although Hendon is quite near to London we had no opportunity to see the metropolis as we were confined to billets for security reasons. We had an easy first week except for the officer and senior NCOs who were being put through their paces it seemed. Then, on the Sunday afternoon at the weekend we received our fortnight leave passes and travel warrants and next day we were off home with dire threats about being hush, hush.

My mother and stepfather were living at Liston near Cambridge at the time and were employed by Chivers Farms. The farm was noted for its production of preserves and fruit and was very famous in that respect. They lived in quite a nice semi-detached house and the estate foreman lived next door. Perce often said that this was the best job he ever had as he was in charge of the horses. These were rather special and were kept as show animals and came out on parade at the various country shows. There were several different breeds such as the Suffolk Punch, Clydesdale and many others. Mum had a photograph of Perce standing in front of a pair of Percherons, they were quite massive and he looked very diminutive standing between them and holding their leads.

These animals were treated more like pets for most of the year but when fully harnessed and attached to various types of cart they looked magnificent and splendid. This tradition still goes on at various country shows in eastern England which is a good thing.

It appeared that the manager of the farm had taught my mother a new skill. Because of the war and the men being involved, there was an acute shortage of labour and this farm consisted mainly of fields of fruit trees! So, the art of pruning the trees was something that had to be maintained as home grown food was becoming more and more important. It seemed there was a definite skill to pruning which had to be taught and necessary if the crop yield was to be good. Well it appeared that she mastered this art and for the remainder of the war they were both very gainfully employed.

By sheer coincidence my brother Leslie arrived home on leave during my second week of leave. He was stationed at Lisburn near Belfast and as mentioned before had married Ann, a very devout protestant lady. This was her first visit to our family and we had a very pleasant reunion. Leslie was expecting to go to the Far East which he eventually did.

The leave soon passed and our unit was on the road back to north east Liverpool where we embarked upon a rusty looking freighter called the 'Mooltan'. One wit remarked that at least Jerrys wouldn't be bothered to waste a torpedo on an old hulk like that and fortunately he was right as it turned out.

When finally assembled our convoy was huge and once in motion very ponderous indeed, our ship and several like it was only capable of eight knots per hour so this had to be the set speed. We found ourselves tucked into the shore side for much of the journey and we could see the escort destroyers speeding up and down on the sea ward side like mother hens looking after its chicks. The Bay of Biscay area was kind to us and not many suffered from sea sickness.

Our accommodation, however, was not very luxurious as we were in hammocks somewhere in the depths of the hold. It was stifling down there and if you wanted to leave the area at night you had more or less to crawl under hundreds of suspended bodies. After a few nights the two young Scottish DRs decided to roll up their hammocks and sleep on deck which was strictly forbidden but by lying close to the deck rail and the weather being fine they somehow got away with it.

For the first part of the journey from Liverpool to Gibraltar we had the additional escort of the two aircraft carriers 'Eagle' and 'Illustrious' and no doubt their spotter aircraft added to our safety. There were some skirmishes and losses during the early weeks of our journey but these were mainly at night. The carriers left our convoy somewhere near Gibraltar and we assumed they had headed into the Mediterranean Sea.

Once we had passed this area things became more relaxed and we began to journey down the west coast of Africa. We changed into our tropical clothes and it felt like a holiday trip for a while! We anchored off Freetown for one night and the view from our boat with the myriad lights on shore looked quite wondrous. The sailors on board thought otherwise as they referred to Freetown as the arsehole of the world and a place never to go near and for us there was very little hope of that anyway.

Idyllic though things seemed we still had to contend with tragedy and I still feel horrified by it to this day. A young soldier, not one of our unit, while hanging out some washing to dry on one of the hold hatches slipped and fell to the bottom of the boat and was killed instantly. How terrible the news of his death must have been to his relatives with him not even getting to his dangerous destination.

We soon found ourselves rounding the Cape of Good Hope and although the sea was rough it was not as bad as we had expected. I don't remember any serious cases of sea sickness throughout the journey which I suppose was quite remarkable.

Another one of the defining things in my life was about to happen which no doubt influenced the next four years of my life.

It was common knowledge that the convoy and its contents was bound to support the North African campaign that was at the time too-ing and fro-ing against the Africa corps. That was our destination but fate was about to take a hand! Somewhere around South Africa our craft developed a propeller problem and during the night tugs from Durban had to come to our rescue and tow us into the harbour. The convoy steamed on and to our delight we awoke that morning in the compound of a wonderland.

We were unloaded and billeted in tents on Clarewood sands while repairs were to take place on the now lovely old 'Mooltan'. To see the locals dressed for summer with the girls and ladies in flimsy dresses seemed so strange, after the dismal coupon regime that we had left in England. The stalls were loaded with fruits that had almost been forgotten about and the whole atmosphere seemed magical.

We were brought down to realities when we were informed by a local army officer that our tents had recently been vacated by a South African division that was on its way to the fighting in North Africa.

We were in Durban for three weeks during which time it had been decided that repairs to the 'Mooltan' had not been possible and stores including ours had been unloaded onto to Quay and we were to wait until other transport arrived.

We were of course still restricted to army routine which included PT at 7 o'clock and we made several route marches to a local beach called Issipingo (I will always remember the name) which was about eight miles along the coast. Once we had left Durban itself these marches became informal, and we were allowed to take swimming gear so a good time was had by all.

During the three weeks we were able to attend a race meeting at Clairwood race track and it seemed great to see the horses and the jockeys in their racing colours.

Good things had of course to come to an end and one evening we were told to be ready to depart early next day.

Having been lined up on the quay in close proximity to our transport and other stores we were amazed to see the trench liner the 'Ile De France' steam in. We were loaded onto the top deck with the many other units in record time and the great ship was turned round and on her way. We did the journey from Durban to Port Tewfik in five days unescorted which seemed amazing after the long eight knots per hour from England to South Africa.

On arrival at Port Tewfik we received orders that seemed quite contrary to our expectations. We assumed that because Germany and her forces were making such rapid inroads against the Russians that re thinking by the allies had taken place.

It was apparently thought at the time that if the Russians collapsed that the German war machine could infiltrate the rich Middle East oilfields near the Balkan countries and Turkey. This indeed seemed feasible at the time.

We as a unit found ourselves not travelling through Egypt to the North African theatre of war but heading across the Syrian desert towards the Lebanon and Syria.

At the desert approach our convoy formed up as we had when travelling in England and I found myself with another DR at the rear. The road was metalled and had quite a reasonable surface with the desert stretching to the horizon on both sides. There were no walls, fences or other wind breaks on either side which meant that our progress was often halted by sand that the wind had drifted onto the road. This was quite deep at times and the cable linesmen who had spades as part of their equipment were frequently called into action to clear a passage.

The heat during this journey was almost unbearable but we knew that this was something we were going to have to endure for an indefinite future.

About half way across the Syrian desert one of the DR's at the front got a puncture. This turned out to be caused by sand getting past the tyre rim and so wearing a hole in the inner tube. The officer, our officer, whose name was Lieutenant Knight decided that I would stay behind with the stricken DR, and assist him with repairing the puncture while the convoy went on. The ideal thing would have been to replace the inner tube with a new one but we were not given that option. We knew that however well we patched the tube that the heat of the sun would affect the adhesive and thus further problems would ensue. We did wonder at the time whether the officer was testing our resourcefulness so we decided to fold a gas cape and fix it over the wheel to at least partly keep the heat off. This seemed to work and we were not too long in catching the struggling convoy so altogether we were quite pleased with ourselves.

The other despatch rider involved was called Fred Hack and he and I were to become quite friendly during the following years. We had a few things in common, we liked reading and music and we found that we were both good card players. Our six despatch riders had really fallen into three pairs, the two young Scots lads, Livingston and McLuiggan got on reasonably well and were going to have to curb their wild ways which eventually did happen. The other two were considerably older, one whose name was Beatley was an introverted, intellectual type of man who seemed out of place. He coped with the job over the next few years which after all was what really mattered. The other DR was an elderly Irishman called Baines who was an older soldier type. He was a pain in many ways and had this idea that with his long service he should at least be a corporal and in charge. He knew, really, that DRs while doing their normal field work did not get promotion. He only had the standard DR III rating which meant in fact that he was subordinate to an inexperienced sprog like me.

To get back to our journey through the Syrian desert! During my four subsequent years in the Middle East I carried a Kodak box camera and during that time took many pictures which I still have in my collection. I have one of Fred and I repairing the puncture or rather of Fred doing the job. That little camera was a miracle really as many of the photographs I have are still clear and not faded with age as perhaps I am.

One other thing I remember on that journey which still seems remarkable happened while our little convoy had stopped for a brew up. Over the sand dunes appeared a small band of Arabs in their flowing white robes and they were offering new laid chicken eggs in exchange for bully beef.

From where we were we could not see habitation or tents and yet they were being quite friendly and seriously business like. I am not too sure of the outcome of these transactions but I am sure that an egg broken on the top of my petrol tank would have been fried in seconds!

I have a feeling those Arabs we encountered were of the travelling type, probably Bedouins and had done similar trading with troops before.

Eventually we arrived at the service area at the far end of the Syrian desert and were able to replenish our petrol supplies. I cannot remember too much detail of all this but we did end up very near Beir Sheba and we spent the night in an empty corrugated tin barn.

An order came from our officer that there would be a parade before departure next morning which would include a short talk followed by an arms inspection.

It was at this point that I did a foolish thing. I cleaned and oiled my revolver and had the foresight to check and clean the six bullets that had been carried in a walking pouch. When removing the bullets from the gun I stupidly left one in the weapon so that when I pulled the trigger to clear the revolving cylinder I fired a shot through the tin roof of the barn. This could have had dire consequences and not only for the obvious reasons but fortunately there were no NCOs present in the barn at that time but the expressions on the faces of the other lads was comic to behold. It took me several months to get a replacement for that bullet as I had to come up with a reasonable excuse to the storeman for its absence.

At the parade next morning we were told that our destination was to be Beirut in the Lebanon so we still had a long journey before us. On the way we were able to visit Nazareth and actually went into the Garden of Gethsemane. This was quite an experience but in all our two and a half years in that area I was never able to visit Jerusalem which I feel was a great shame.

For the next two and a half years we were stationed at Beirut, we were attached to 241 Wing RAF and we were their main signals HQ. For the first few weeks we were actually on the airport itself but after a few air raids had taken place our signals HQ was moved to a large empty house about a mile away. Our teleporters and radios were soon housed there and our linesman busy putting in the necessary cables. We then realized how lucky we had become with this move as the house was quite large with suitable buildings to house our transport and motorcycles. There was also a big bonus insomuch as there was a rocky passage at the back that led down to the sea.

After a few weeks and when well established and organised, our off duty personnel, usually those that had been on night duty could just wander down to the beach and sleep and recuperate there.

The weather was at least ninety per cent good, the sea was warm and buoyant and it was a good place to be. I found that after a few weeks I could swim quite well, something I could not do before and was able to swim out several hundred yards to a moored raft.

As army personnel we were very shabbily dressed compared to our RAF counterparts. This was very evident at our first combined parade on the airfield. The RAF boys including RAF regiment personnel had shoes, long socks, proper shorts and nice shirts and looked quite splendid. Our officer it must be said also looked very resplendent but not so his merry men! I suppose it is true to say that we had originally been intended to be in the North African campaign where our boaters and shorter socks and coarse shirts would have been more appropriate. Our shorts were the worst feature and they looked quite ghastly, they were designed to fold down and fit into our socks to keep out mosquitoes and other insects so when buttoned up for normal use they looked very baggy and unsightly. Things did improve with time and with a bit of bargaining between stores we were able to wangle the odd pair of shorts but of course army issue had to be kept intact and kit checks were often the order of the day.

During those early weeks in the Lebanon and Syria things were quite strange. The territory had been French mandated before the war and it was difficult to know at the time who favoured the Vichy regime and who were De Gaullists.

I can remember having to take a special despatch from Beirut to Damascus. This was for the free French HQ there and was most secret and most immediate as most specials were! Our officer came out from our signals office and handed it to me with a caution to make sure that it got to the right place as there were suspected subversise elements in Damascus. As it turned out I had no problems and the free French HQ was quite prominent and central in the city.

The ride from Beirut to Damascus takes one up through the mountains and also embraces the beautiful cedar trees of the Lebanon. The road winds upwards for several miles and includes many hairpin bends and unfenced stretches and the view from up there looking down on Beirut was really stunning. One could see the airfield at one end and the harbour at the other all fringed by the deep Mediterranean Sea.

I did not see much of this on the way up as I had to concentrate on my mission but on the way back I was able to relax and enjoy quite an unforgettable experience. On one of the severe corners was a massive advertising boarding of the Michelin tyre man! Most people will know of this French type advert as I believe the company still owns it. I had been told by other despatch riders that it was customary to put a bullet from their revolvers through this large metal man on the way down and sure enough it was possible to see numerous holes through it.

So being young and full of high spirits I did the same and not giving too much thought as to how I would be able to replace the missing ammo. Well, you do daft things when young and we were living through extraordinary times!

Our first year which embraced most of 1941 was relatively quiet at Beirut. At this time the Americans had not yet entered the war and it seemed the Germans and Italians were reluctant to bomb the airfield as there were many Americans in the area. The American University was still in full flow and was situated at the opposite side of the city to the airport, nearer the harbour. This made bombing rather tricky so I suppose this was a lucky break for us. Our duties at the time embraced the other RAF units on the airstrip and they tended to keep us quite busy. Their Air Sea Rescue unit, being so close to the action on the Med, was often in action and we had a DR on standby for the full 24 hours. There was also a photograph reconnaissance unit on the strip which consisted of specially equipped Spitfires. These were very busy people and it was quite dangerous work for the pilots. There was an MU (maintenance unit) there as well so we did have our hands full at times.

The temperatures for the most part were quite high but we did benefit from the breezes from the sea. Sleeping conditions were not good and bed bugs were quite a hazard. I slept for most of the time on a wooden stretcher that slotted together and frequently doused the whole thing in petrol and by quickly running a blowtorch along the structure the verminous creatures could be removed. When this was done the smell was awful but at least you had a few good nights until the creatures colonised again.

It was about this time that I caught impetigo which came out on my hands and face and was quite nasty and painful. When I went to the RAF sick bay with this I was rather surprised to find that the only other patient with this malady was the MO himself. He was treating the spots with a yellow powdery cream called pasta flava and soon we were both looking like red Indians. Well, I got the same treatment as he did which I am sure was the best available at the time. After a few days we progressed to a treatment that was called 'blue unction' and that also looked pretty horrible.

In time it cleared up and considering that impetigo is quite contagious it was a wonder that other people didn't get it!

For quite a time we had a settled routine and our signals HQ functioned very well. The routine despatch work for us was like a quick postal service and our DR runs embraced the forces units for a wide area. There were naval quarters at the docks and a barrage balloon unit that protected to some extent the local population.

Fred Hack and I had become quite friendly and often shared the 24 hour standby stint which allowed the other riders to do the routine runs. The night duty could be a bore but the one on duty could use the rest room although as one had to remain fully clothed with riding kit handy it was not really restful. Our main call out was to take urgent signals to the duty pilot on the airstrip and often they were to do with air sea rescue operations.

After we had been at Beirut for about eighteen months, and when the African campaign moved further east, a few of us were sent on detachment to Aleppo in Northern Syria. The RAF had a newly acquired radar station which was becoming important as at the time the Russians were in full retreat and there was real danger that the Germans could eventually gain an entrance to the Iranian airfields by the route through Turkey. The detachment was quite small and consisted of four radio ops, four linesmen and two DRs. We were to become part of 63 operating unit and came under their jurisdiction for our welfare and a senior sergeant was in charge overall.

The journey from the Lebanon to Aleppo was just about one hundred miles and was not particularly scenic! It did, however, pass through the large towns of Hama and Hims which were quite busy places and typical of the Arab way of life. The skyline at Hama was dominated by a massive waterwheel which we could see when approaching the town. This apparently irrigated a large area. Even today I am not sure how it was driven but being quite close to the road it seemed massive as we rode past it.

The airstrip when we arrived turned out to be a few miles north of Aleppo and was called Neirab. The only planes there on a permanent basis were Free French and the R.A.F. presence was mainly to do with communications.

It turned out to be a very pleasant assignment for us as our duties were not too severe. There was even a rather run-down tennis court that we were allowed to use. There was quite an all round social attitude when we first arrived and we played football as a mixed R.A.F.-Army team against other units stationed in the area. I can remember there being Whist drives and even musical evenings but unfortunately things were soon going to take a downturn.

The radar mast and a small station were away from the main buildings as maximum air clearance was desired for effective turnings. The station was manned for the full twenty-four hours and at night an operator was always on duty.

The dreadful thing was that the young operator was murdered. You could hardly call it an act of war as he was simply shot out of hand, callously. It was found to be that the gun used was probably a weapon from the First World War as the extracted bullet suggested this. It was assumed that the crime was perpetrated by an anti-De Gaullist Arab who then just disappeared into the night.

This led to a general tightening up all round. Guard duties were doubled and we found ourselves part of this and there was an air of dejection everywhere.

There were several young W.A.A.F. officers on the station and we as part of the signals unit came into contact with them as we manned the telephone exchange. I was on this extra guard duty one night patrolling the transport area and in the vicinity of the H.Q. building when I heard wonderful music coming from one of the windows. It was the Mendelssohn violin concerto and in the stillness of the night to me it sounded so beautiful. I had never heard it before and it seemed like an awakening to me and an introduction to another world.

On enquiring the next day about this I was told that one of the W.A.A.F. officers had a collection of 78rpm classical records and it must have been from that source that the music had come.

It was also on one of these guard duties that I reached my twenty-first birthday and not one person except me realised this. On the other hand I cannot remember celebrating anyone else's birthday in those troubled times so perhaps that was not so unusual.

We were on this detachment for about eight months and generally we were having things easy! I remember being on duty for one special dispatch in which I got lost and inadvertently crossed the Turkish border. I found myself in a massive cemetery which seemed to go on forever and on rounding a sharp corner I knocked over an Arab of some sort. The Army policy was quite clear on these matters and if an accident occurred while on duty you did not stop but carried on regardless. This may seem rather heartless but we were at war and I was in fact in a seemingly neutral country so consequences could have been awkward if there had been an official enquiry. At the same time the situation with the Turks was not at all clear as it was well known that we had personnel in that country dressed as civilians and the numbers were reputed to be quite high.

I eventually got back on track and delivered the dispatch and the journey was roughly towards the Iran border where the allies had many troops at the time because of the importance of the oilfields.

I still have horrors about that large cemetery and have often wondered why it was so large! I remember from my history lessons at school that somewhere in that area there was once a huge massacre of Armenians and I have often wondered if that could have been some associated burial place but I cannot be sure of this.

That stay at Neirab (Aleppo) brought about my longest dispatch run in my army career. I was awoken at about two o'clock in the morning and told to get ready to take messages and a field telephone to Lattakia which I knew was on the eastern coast of the Mediterranean Sea. It appeared that landline communication had been lost somehow so this was an important assignment. The field telephone, which was contained in a box, was quite a heavy instrument and when I got to my bike our sergeant and an R.A.F. officer were already fixing this contraption to the tank. It was on a cloth pad and strapped in place and I remember them saying that to strap it on the back over the wheel would have caused damage although, to me, that would have been the most logical place to have put it. Well, it turned out to be a very uncomfortable ride, I knew the route to Lattakia seemed fairly straightforward on the map and as it turned out it was well signposted. The road, however, was poor in parts and it was not possible to go fast so steady progress was maintained. The large protrusion on the tank certainly did not help and I remember arriving at the R.A.F. H.Q. in Lattakia with some relief. This, however, was short lived as after delivering the dispatches and given a hurried meal I was told that the telephone was destined for a unit further up the coast. This turned out to be a small friendly M.U. and they were pleased to get the phone as they had been isolated for some considerable time.

Well, that was the important part of the mission completed and I was offered a sort of B&B before the return journey began towards home. On completion of this I had clocked over 430 miles and was looking forward to a few days of recuperation.

We were rather sad to leave Neirab as we had made some good friends with the lads from 68 Operating Unit and also the R.A.F. boys. We had our orders to return to Beirut and we were soon back at our usual duties.

Although we were never shooting at Germans or they shooting at us directly, death and tragedy were never far away and came so unexpectedly. After a night of duty the people off shift, which included myself, went down to the beach as usual for a swim and a rest. One of our number was a rather tubby man who was a teleprinter operator and in fact a very competent swimmer. He decided to do some diving from a fairly low crop of rocks which most of us had done before without problems. We were watching from the beach and after a dive he floated up face down flapping his arms and legs in a peculiar way and we thought he was just being funny and arsing about. After this went on for a short time we realised that something was amiss and dragged him out onto some towels on the beach. It became apparent that all was not well with him and a runner was sent to our H.Q. for help. An ambulance eventually arrived with a stretcher party and the difficult job of getting this heavy man up the rocky pathway began.

It appeared that when diving from the rocks that he had hit his head on a sandbank in the sea and has broken his neck. The hospital staff at first gave him a fifty-fifty chance of survival but he did not make it. I suppose the delay and the nature of his rescue up the cliff did not help.

For many months after this happened we had the job of returning his mail as it was part of our DR duties to pick up our letters and parcels from the Army P.O. It seemed so sad and awful for his folks back home for his life to have been lost in this way.

In February 1944 we received orders to leave Syria and we were told that we would be heading for a coastal destination in North Africa. Our unit was still a full wing signals section and we assumed we would be backing up a bomber wing as before.

The war at the time had moved on from North Africa to Italy, and I knew that brother Gordon was still very much involved in the tank battles that were going on. Our journey was well over a thousand miles and we were fortunate to have a few days in a transit camp at El Giza. We would see the Pyramids in the distance when we arrived and were lucky enough to have a closer view of them and the Sphinx during our stay.

On we went in our small convoy towards the African coast and we had an overnight stay on the main coastal road near El Alamein. I remember walking over to this edge and the sight of the thousands of graves was really awe-inspring. The Graves Commission Unit was still busy bringing in bodies from the battlefields and I suppose there will still be many casualties that were never found or identified in that area. I think today how lucky we were that that old freighter broke down on our journey round the Cape. It could well have altered our destiny as we were originally bound for that campaign.

By this time we had been told that our destination was the airfield at Benina which proved to be about nine miles inland from Benghazi. Further along the coast from El Alamein I had my only mechanical breakdown with an army machine. The oil pump situated at the bottom of the engine gave out suddenly and caused the problem. There was a spare bike on the three-ton truck used by the linesmen, so I was soon mounted again. I was glad that this happened to me on convoy duty and not on a dispatch rider delivery as that could have been much more serious.

Several nights during this journey we slept in the open and realised how cold the desert became at night and also very uncomfortable sleeping on the sand.

When reaching Benina we took over from another communication unit, so things for us were soon established. At first quite a few bombers were using the airstrip in support of the bloody battle that was going on in Italy on the other side of the Med, but after a few months the situation for us became quiet and fairly routine. We had to support a large H.Q. in Benghazi where there were Army, Naval as well as R.A.F. personnel and our duties were delivering dispatches to them and other units situated along the coast.

I can remember riding through locust storms on several occasions which proved to be an unpleasant experience. Provided you had protective clothing with goggles up and mouth closed you just weathered the plague like a hailstorm. The problem of scraping these creatures from a very hot engine afterwards was a very debilitating and smelly procedure.

As DRs we found ourselves involved in other duties at this time and I had quite an unusual experience when on the telephone exchange on a comparatively quiet Sunday afternoon. If you opened a line by lifting a lever and whistled into the headset you got the tune coming almost stereophonically back through the headphones! I was doing this in a sort of bored way when an educated lady's voice suddenly came on the line. It said, "That was a very nice rendering of Gounod's Ave Maria but would you mind putting me through to the Wing Commander who is my husband, as I have an important message for him."

I expected there would be some serious comeback from this via our officer but she must have been a kindly lady and I had no adverse telling off.

The two senior sergeants in the unit had been with us since the section formed at Colwyn Bay in 1940. They were both very good at their jobs, one was overall in charge after the officer and the other in charge of the operators which comprised the bulk of our numbers, being in charge of the teleprinters and wireless procedures. They were both ardent cricketers and since one was from Yorkshire and the other Lancashire there was a great deal of friendly rivalry. During our two years in the Lebanon our unit had had a nucleus of a cricket team. It had consisted of mainly the NCOs and hangers-on and it never seemed to be very successful. In my opinion the climatic conditions were against it. I was never asked to play and under the old adage of 'don't volunteer for anything' I preferred to spend my spare time either reading or on the beach when the weather permitted.

Having said all that, I was rather surprised when one evening at Benina I was called over by one of these sergeants and handed a cricket ball. I had noticed that a few of the unit spent some evenings practising against the end of one of the huts where the ground, although just a mud strip, was very level and hard. I remember him muttering about me being an unsociable git and didn't do much except ride my bloody motorbike, and how about bowling a few balls and joining in.

I was 22 at the time and having yanked 380lb motorcycles about for over four years I was probably as fit then as I have ever been in my life. However, my cricket experiences had been limited to a few games at school and an occasional foray on the village green at Gt. Chishill so I was to all aspects an unknown quantity. The Lancastrian sergeant was at the wicket when I began my run-up and the ball hurtled towards his head at according to them, "a really fast rate". I remember him remonstrating at me with his fists and then calmly explaining where on the pitch I should be aiming. Well, it seems that it was then considered by experts that I was potentially a very quick bowler and if they could harness this raw talent then all could be well!

A few weeks later I remember playing for the unit team against a team from the sergeants' mess. Apparently there were some good cricketers amongst the R.A.F. sergeants and our sergeants, who of course were playing for us, must have thought we could give them a good game.

In the event we lost the game as our batting was poor but I managed to take six of the opposing wickets which included two batsmen who were considered very good, so what price fame at last!

We were at Benina for almost six months and once again the war had moved away from us and in early 1944 we were disbanded. I became lucky again and found that I was to be posted to the British Embassy in Cairo as a DR and courier. This turned out to be a plum job and an entirely new aspect and routine from the normal army way of life. It was like a different world in almost every way and I found myself billeted in a spacious sun room in the Embassy grounds. There were three other DRs who had been there for some time and they were riding the latest Matchless motorcycles with telescopic forks and other latest innovations and it seemed all too good to be true.

Our main work was fairly local as we were delivering dispatches to the other Embassies and delegations in Cairo and it was fairly straightforward and routine. This was made more difficult as the City was getting unaccustomed rain showers at the time which turned the roads into ice rinks. The accumulation of engine oil on the streets after the long hot months when mixed with rainwater caused a dangerous slime to form which was very hazardous.

The cars at the Embassy were Rolls-Royces and we were billeted with an Army chauffeur and a local Egyptian one so we got to know them well. They were of course very well turned out and handpicked for the job.

While at the Embassy I had a surprise visit from brother Gordon who was on leave from the tank battles in Italy. It was such a surprise but he seemed so different from the young farm lad I had known before the war. The war had certainly taken its toll but in spite of that he seemed quite cheerful. I still have a photograph of us both together taken at the time.

We still had one grim reminder that the war was far from over as an Egyptian courier while carrying official dispatches from Cairo to Alexandria was murdered on the train and the bag stolen.

I imagine that he was armed but details were vague and this affected us as we were detailed to take over this run. It seemed strange carrying dispatches by train in a first-class compartment with a loaded weapon but these were very evil times.

There was a pet dog in the from of a Great Dane that belonged on the premises. It was a cuddly soppy animal called Simba, no use at all as a watchdog, but just part of the establishment. There was also a rather ancient motorcycle there in the form of a V-Twin B.S.A. 1000cc which was also part of the setup. I remember this particularly as I took a photograph with my Brownie box camera of one of the DRs holding this dog on the motorcycle with its paws on the handlebars and I still have this in my collection of snaps.

My four-year spell as a soldier in the Middle East came to an end in November 1944. During that time I had had no home leave and was due for repatriation. Today soldiers serving in wars abroad serve only six months and then get a stirring welcome home. They also have the luxury of a comfortable flight home.

On our return, and there were many of us, we crossed the Mediterranean sea by cargo boat which stood off Valletta harbour, Malta for three days. Then we disembarked at Toulon in Southern France and crossed Europe to Dieppe by train in little more than cattle trucks.

Looking back on that it all seems pretty harsh but I suppose we were young, tough and just grateful that we had survived and at last were on our way home.

One last thing that happened at the Embassy, was in the form of an offer to return and become some form of civil servant. This was tempting as staff were needed and training and promotion almost promised. In the end I decided that four years in the area was enough but often wonder how things in my life would have changed if I had taken up that offer.

When we arrived at Dieppe and started our crossing to Newhaven the seas in the Channel were mountainous with a severe gale blowing. A friendly sailor told us that to avoid seasickness it was best to find a high point on the boat deck and keep as still as possible. We were also feeling the cold as it was November 1944 and our tropical sojourn had left us with thin blood. We took the sailor's advice and stayed under the lifeboats wrapped in our army greatcoats and just about staved off Mal de Mer but it was a very uncomfortable ride.

The Royal Signals personnel were directed by train to our holding battalion near Huddersfield and here I had an unexpected surprise waiting. I was directed to a different queue in the orderly room and told if I signed the necessary papers I could be released from the army straight away on a class B release. It seemed that this applied to certain people who had trade experience and as I had been in building before the war I qualified.

It was pointed out that my proper army release was not due under class A for several months and that I would have to report to Coulson and Son, my previous employers, and work for them for that period. My signature for this commitment was required and failure to comply meant a return to the services. So after picking up my de-mob suit (an awful grey pinstripe) I shed my army shackles and returned home after five and a half years.

From Twenty-Five to Thirty

My mother and stepfather were still living at Histon and working for Chivers' Farms. She had spent the war using her spare time pruning fruit trees and he was still in charge of the show horses and their regalia and they seemed quite content with their lot.

It was a quiet welcome home and as I had fourteen days paid leave I was able to get organised before reporting for work. I had made an allowance from my army pay and my mother had been putting this in a savings account for my return but even so it had only accumulated about sixty pounds. As transport was essential I embarked on a visit to London to buy a suitable motorcycle. There was a firm called Pride and Clarke that advertised a lot in the 'Motorcycle' before the war and so I bought a 250cc Triumph machine from them which swallowed up most of my savings. It was quite a nice little machine and suited my purpose well enough.

When I reported for work eventually I was in for a shock. The busy workshops that I had known were dark and empty, and the machine shop also non-functional. The only person about was the elderly stoneman who had been there before hostilities and seemed to be the only retainer. He told me that he thought that it would be months and perhaps years before things returned to normal. The only work they had was erecting Swedish pre-fabricated houses at Duxford and I would report there next morning. So on a miserable foggy November morning I made the journey to Duxford which I knew was about ten miles or so from Histon and reported to the site foreman. He was quite friendly but pointed out that until the concrete bases and the assembly of the sections of these houses was done there would be no work for carpenters, let alone joiners. I would in fact, it appeared, be a labourer until that happened which could take weeks.

I stuck with this situation until the Friday of that week and then told the office that I intended to report back to the army forthwith as I had no intention of being a building labourer.

During my time in the Middle East I had had a pen relationship with a young lady called Joan South. Her parents and mine were quite friendly before the war so I got to know her quite well from the age of sixteen. They lived at Enfield in North London and Joan seemed to need some connection with the war as her parents were too old to participate and having got my address from my home she wrote to me quite frequently for all the time I was overseas. I suppose we had some romantic notions in all this as that was the way it was during those torrid times. Her parents were comparatively well off and had a fur business situated on the Thames with workshops and warehouses, and their house at Enfield was quite on the grand scale. Joan, being an only daughter, had a lifestyle that was better than most but nevertheless she was a nice person and quite unspoiled.

Before contacting the army I decided to visit Joan and her parents in Enfield. I had an open invitation, so on that Friday evening I set off on the bike to stay for the weekend. They were all very welcoming and on the Sunday we went for a car drive into the country to Epping Forest with Joan and I in a cuddling situation in the back. When we returned to their home later that afternoon her father was reading the local paper which, it seemed, had in it an advertisement for carpenters and joiners to work for Edmonton County Council. He suggested that I stay one more night and on the Monday I should make enquiries at the site for employment. He pointed out that they had a room that I could occupy and it seemed a possible solution to my problems at the time.

The foreman at the building site was a middle-aged sympathetic sort of man, especially towards servicemen, and it appeared that he had a son who was in a similar position who would soon be ex-R.A.F. He said that they were desperately short of skilled men and could I start the next day. There were several houses that were ready for the internal woodwork to be done so it would be inside work. This entailed fitting doors, locks, architraves, skirting etc. and included fitting the staircase and various cupboards so it was quite good quality work required.

I pointed out that my army commitment was to the firm in Cambridge but he assured me that provided I was working in the building construction work that there would be no problem with the War Department.

It meant travelling home to Histon to pick up clothes, tools and belongings and to explain the situation to Mother and then back to Enfield to start work on the Thursday.

I found myself in the position of fitting out a house by myself which was fine. After a day or two the foreman came in accompanied by the Clerk of Works to see my progress. They seemed satisfied enough but suggested that I should work on a self-employed basis which meant that I could work more houses and be paid a set rate for each completed house instead of an hourly rate. I decided against this as I thought I would become bound to a life of grind and excessive hard work. After five years for King and country I felt I had earned some degree of freedom and enjoyment.

There was also a worrying factor about my association with Joan and her parents. They were very nice people and had treated me well but I had come to realise that if I married Joan I could never keep her in the life to which she had been accustomed. Being an only daughter she had been carefully nurtured all her life and just simply used to a fairly extravagant lifestyle. She was employed by her father's firm and I think she did some office work or packaging and generally made herself useful so that she travelled to London with her father and had a fairly stress-free life and seemed quite happy with that.

I had been staying with them and working for Edmonton County Council for about six months when matters came to a head. I usually got to the house before Joan and her father as they were often held up by traffic even in those days of 1946. It was Friday and when I arrived after work I saw on the back of the chair several garments and pinned to them was a bill from a dry cleaning firm. I was looking at this when Joan's mum came in and she said that they had arrived back that day. The amount on the bill was almost half of what I earned in a week and I pointed this out to her mum – she just said that Joan, as I knew, liked to keep herself smart and that was just a fact.

Later that evening after our meal I decided to put my thoughts to Joan and her folk. I pointed out that if we went ahead and got engaged I would no doubt be able to get a council house as I was a settled employee of the E.C.C. but also that I would want to be a proper husband and provider and this would entail an independent life. I suggested that Joan and I had a quiet discussion about this and what it would entail. Her father, who was a thoughtful and considerate man, seemed to think it to be a good idea but I could see that both Joan and her mother were completely taken aback.

Left to our own devices Joan said how pleased she was that I had made up my mind about an engagement! She, however, could see an austere life in front of her and could see no reason why we could not continue as we were! She pointed out that eventually the house would be hers and that she would be quite wealthy. I pointed out that her parents were comparatively young and that I wanted her to join me in an independent life and that was how it would have to be. This of course brought tears and temper to the scene and all went to bed in a fraught and unhappy atmosphere.

On the Saturday morning we still had hostile feelings so I suggested to Joan that we had a few weeks' separation to see how things developed. Her parents seemed to think this a good idea as they realised that Joan was not at all happy.

At this time my elder sister Doreen and her husband Dennis had been settled in Chelmsford for some time. He was still employed in the butchery trade and worked in a shop in Moulsham Street in the St. John's area of Chelmsford. They had a twelve-year-old son called Michael and seemed to be quite settled there.

I had been down to see them on the odd occasion from Enfield on my motorcycle and I was fairly sure that they would put me up in their spare room on a temporary basis if I asked them.

So on the Monday morning I gathered my few belongings together and left Churchbury Lane, Enfield. I called in at the builders' office at Edmonton and explained the situation to the friendly foreman who seemed very sorry to lose a good worker but being a reasonable sort of man he seemed to understand! I told him that I could be back if matters improved and after getting my employment cards and gathering my woodworking tools I departed for Chelmsford. My motorcycle panniers were rather over-laden but I managed to get to my sister's abode at Nursery Road in Chelmsford without too much difficulty.

She didn't seem too surprised to see me and was quite welcoming, we had always got on well together. I remember handing over my food coupons as at the time in 1946 food rationing was still very much the order of the day. Her spare room in their rented house was very small and the bed took up most of the space, still I was very grateful to her and Dennis for putting me up! I suppose for them it was like a break from their normal routine which I guess was fairly mundane.

The son was at Moulsham Secondary Modern School and I think that they were quite proud of him. At the time he had been selected to sing a small solo part for boy soprano in Felix Mendelssohn's Elijah which was being put on by the local operatic society. Mick quietly confided to me that he hated the idea as he was losing face with his contemporaries but in the event the performance went very well and he did his part very well also.

The school at Moulsham was to become quite important to me in the next few years although at the time I was not aware of this. I had no difficulty in getting a job with a local firm who were known as Selwoods and Company. After a few months I found myself helping to put up pre-fabricated workshops and domestic science rooms at Moulsham School. This was contracted work from the Essex Education Committee and the firm also had similar contracts at Rainsford School which was situated on the other side of Chelmsford from Moulsham. In the meantime I had joined the local motorcycle club and was beginning to find life more interesting.

Joan's parents had meanwhile been down one week and it seemed that I had been missed! On that particular day I was not in

Chelmsford as the Motorcycle Club had an outing to see a speedway match at West Ham in London and I had gone with them.

My sister must have told them that I had settled down in the area and that was the last I heard of them. It was probably for the best in the long run although I little knew of the awful problems that were to be mine in later life.

Activities at the Club were restricted very much by petrol rationing and at the time we had competitions on bicycles. On one occasion I borrowed Dennis' sit up and beg cycle and took part in a trials competition. The bike had large 28" wheels and high handlebars and this combination suited the rough trials course very well and I somehow won the event. The results were even in the local paper so fame had come at last!

The club was also a family affair as there were several members who had motorcycles with sidecars attached and wives and children went with them. Two brothers whose name I think was Ransome were quite well-to-do farmers who had an interest in motorcycle racing. They both owned Manx racing Nortons which although not the latest models were quite fast machines. They usually prepared these bikes and raced them in the Isle of Man T.T.s which provided us and the locality with an interest.

It seemed they planned their holidays around these events as their wives travelled with them. Other club members also went as assistants as everything had to be well organised.

They never managed to be successful in the races as by this time the multi-cylinder machines from Italy, Germany and Japan were beginning to be in the ascendancy and of course still are.

The club was very popular and attracted a number of young women, some who had boyfriends with motorcycles and other adventurous types that hoped for rides to the various venues that the club went to! There were various other non-motorcycle activities such as darts and table tennis and the girls helped to keep refreshments going, so there was quite a communal atmosphere all round. As I had no feminine attachment at the time I frequently had a pillion passenger and after several months formed an attachment to one particular girl and eventually got engaged and later got married!

Her name was Joyce Wiseman and she lived with her parents in a council house in Chelmsford. Her father worked a drilling machine at Crompton Parkinsons factory and had done so for many years. She had a brother who was a bit younger than she was and he was in the process of going to live with relatives in Canada so I never really got to know him very well.

Her mother was a very quiet, homely woman and they both made me very welcome. Each Sunday as regular as clockwork (as they say) she caught a bus to Southend-on-Sea apparently to visit an old friend who was a priest. He lived alone and I expect she did his weekly chores and suchlike but Joyce herself always gave me the impression that there was more than a friendly thing going on between them.

From Twenty-Five to Thirty

When eventually we married we had a quiet wedding at Southend-on-Sea and the service was taken by the priest friend of the mother-in-law and all seemed well.

The winter of 1947-8 was probably the worst during the whole of that century and proceeded in a deep freezing, foggy atmosphere from October to the following March. It just went on and on and had a devastating effect on everyone and particularly the building trade.

I was working on a small building site at the time and early in October after several days of severe frost our whole workforce with the exception of two were laid off. The head of the firm had decided that he would keep one bricklayer and one joiner. The idea was that with any temporary improvement in the weather some work could be done in this way. The bricklayer was a family man with two children and he lived in the Rainsford area of Chelmsford with his wife. They had a bungalow with quite a large mortgage so he was very relieved to still have a job. His name was Stan Hart and he was destined to play quite a part in my future. We were quite friendly and he always seemed to be whistling classical tunes. He was a good person to work with but I got the impression that although he was very good at his job he did not like the idea of taking on responsibility.

I was the other worker to be kept on during that awful winter and together with the foreman who was the head man's brother-in-law, we were destined to make ourselves as comfortable as we could and more or less await the Spring.

We put a temporary roof over one of the unfinished rooms and made ourselves a fire from a perforated oil drum and with the windows boarded up we were able to keep warm.

It was about this time in October 1947 when reading an advertisement in the 'Woodworker' magazine that I was to start on an entirely new career strategy which, until reading this advertisement, I had had no thought of pursuing! It seemed that the educational authorities at the time were requiring skilled tradesmen in woodwork or metalwork to train to be teachers in secondary education. On reading further down the page it became apparent that the advertisement itself was put in the 'Woodworker' by Chambers College of Chiselhurst in Kent, who specialised in postal courses.

I decided to send for the prospectus and further details and when they arrived I was surprised how well organised the handicraft teachers' course was. This would be a two-year course, the first year would be the academic work plus a practical exam and a theory paper relating to either choice of woodwork or metalwork.

It stated that a pass had to be attained in all the stated academic subjects during the first year before taking the second year. This entailed two maths papers (pure and applied), two English papers (literature and language) and a general science paper. They made it quite clear that if you failed one of these papers the whole lot would have to be taken in a subsequent year, again. The science paper was interesting as when I eventually started the course the text book supplied was a softback and was divided into sections under headings of heat, light, sound and electricity. I simply carried this book around in my overcoat pocket and read it through and through during that cold winter.

Once I had started this work I found it quite interesting. The cost of the course overall was fairly expensive but the lessons they set were well-prepared in all the subjects and provided I did the work it was quickly marked and returned and I felt I was getting good value for money. The most difficult subject for me was the pure maths paper and even when I eventually took that exam I was far from confident. Finally the examinations had to be taken at the Technical College in Chelmsford and took place over several Saturday mornings.

I was the only candidate for these exams so the invigilator concerned had a rather boring but fairly lucrative few Saturday mornings.

These took place in May. The practical exam was relatively easy for me and the theory of woodwork I found not at all difficult.

So during these months of relative inactivity at the building site I tried to put some of the time to good use. Doing the course, however, was quite hard work, during the evenings and weekends. I was supplied by the college with relevant past papers to take towards the end of the course and these were most helpful and the marks I had were fairly encouraging.

Early in January 1948 and after I had started studying, something happened that I look back on as a very important and lucky break in my life. The director of the firm, who I thought was very kindly disposed towards Stan Hart and myself by keeping us at work during that time, arrived one morning with a surprising proposal. He knew, it seemed, that I was married and lived with in-laws and had probably been told this by our site foreman who was his brother-in-law. He said that because of the lack of activity during the winter he had been unable to use his full quota of building licenses and although he was supposed to hand these back he could and would offer one to me. Now building licenses at the time were like gold dust and what he was saying seemed almost unreal.

He continued by saying that quick action was required and what I would have to do was to purchase a plot of land that was registered. There was apparently a road called Wallace Crescent that had been partly built on before the war, so the road and pavements, drainage water and sewage amenities were in place. He said that if I wanted to take advantage of this offer I would have to see the farmer who owned the land as soon as possible. He was addressing all this to Stan as well as myself and stated that a good idea would be to build a semi-detached bungalow as we would build two more cheaply as one.

Stan would do the brickwork and myself the woodwork and of course the general labouring and other work we would also do.

As this was an offer I could not refuse I made haste to see the farmer who owned the land. He stated the plot next to the last pre-war house would be the one available and the size of frontage was limited by the council to 36ft for a detached dwelling and 52ft for a semi-detached one. The price was £2-10 per foot in old money. The depth of the plot was already determined by the boundary fence in place.

Considering I had no resources, this was going to be some undertaking and although £2-10 seems a ridiculous sum by today's standards it was quite a lot in those days. On consultation with wife and in-laws we could just about raise the ninety pounds required.

The next day when Stan arrived at work he and his wife had decided that although the semi-detached idea was cheating in many respects they would have to stick with their present arrangements as they already had problems with their mortgage and could not afford to complicate their lives further. He assured me, however, that if I went ahead with the scheme that he would do the brickwork and drains and help me when he could and I would pay him at standard brickies' rate of pay. This was a very kind offer on his part as it was obvious that most of the work would have to be done at weekends and evenings when normally he could have expected to earn a higher rate of pay.

A few days later I took the plunge and purchased the designated plot and became the owner of 36ft by 90ft of land. The farmer or one of his workers came and measured the correct frontage and fixed a temporary fence with round poles and bailing wire. I was given a warning about keeping accurately to the building line with the front of the property which I already knew was a strict by-law.

Having procured the plot I had envisaged in my mind a span of at least four years hard work in front of me. I thought it would be a question of earning money before I could spend it on the necessary building materials but this was not to be the case. Over the next few days things began to happen that seemed like manna from heaven or small miracles and in fact there were going to be several of these during the next two years.

I got home from work one evening and mother-in-law told me that the Salvation Army Insurance man had been that day to collect for some small policies that she had with them. She had mentioned the building project and he said that his company had a life insurance policy that could be coupled with a house purchase scheme which might interest me and that he would come round the next evening to discuss this.

He arrived with all the relevant information and the outcome of this meeting was good. The monthly payments were higher than a normal life policy but if I took one out I could borrow £1000 for building purposes. This would be paid in three stages of the building procedure, £300 at ground floor level, £300 at eaves level and the remaining four hundred on completion of the building.

The policy covered my life so that if anything happened to me they would be liable to settle outstanding monies on this. Basically for a set monthly sum which was considerable but not beyond my means they would loan me these stages of money. This was in fact like a mortgage over a twenty year period and was certainly a workable scheme from my point of view.

There were clauses in the contract in so much as they would inspect the work before paying out at each stage. This suited me well enough as that was a guarantee of our workmanship and satisfaction and I had no qualms at all in signing the necessary documents.

This meant of course that I would have to finance the materials used for the first stage of the building. When I got home one evening from work at about this time I had a pleasant surprise waiting. My wife's aunt who lived in Sawbridgeworth, which is on the Essex-Hertfordshire border, had a caring job which included looking after an elderly spinster whose name was Becky or Rebecca Wood. The aunt apparently told this lady of our building enterprise and she must have been very impressed. She apparently had no close relatives, it seemed, and without much hesitation gave the aunt one hundred pounds in cash to help our building endeavours.

She made only one stipulation or request, that the bungalow would be called 'Kenwood', being part of my Christian name and her surname. Once again Lady Luck was on hand to help us and this meant we would have money to buy the initial drain and footing materials to get the project started.

I had already been told by the firm's managing director or my main benefactor that if I contacted his son, who was the architect for the firm, that I could peruse suitable plans for a small bungalow. When I visited his office he showed me several suitable sets of plans, the right size for the plot of land. They were the usual two bedroom setup with a lounge, kitchen and usual amenities and it was just a question of choice! Most of the designs had a gable roof which is the most simple roof to construct and I plumped for one of these. The architect himself suggested that from a visual perspective another design would be better value in the future. It incorporated a hipped roof which would be further complicated by a bay window as part of the lounge. The design on paper certainly looked more attractive than the others on display so I eventually took his advice.

I was a bit concerned as I never had the opportunity to be involved in putting on any sort of roof. My work had always been to do with joinery and roofing came under the category of carpentry. Still, as with most aspects of life, with the aid of common sense I would be able to cope when the time came, I supposed!

I was expecting to pay a fair sum in guineas for these plans as they were expertly presented with a list of materials required to build and also duplicate copies so I could have one set at home and the other set on the building site. I was quite amazed when he said that as they were pre-war plans, he was giving them to me and mumbled that enterprise should be rewarded so and once again I had fallen on my feet.

Over the period of the next two months and working weekends and evenings as these lengthened, Stan and I completed the first stage of the bungalow. We dug foundation trenches and concreted them by hand, laid the drains, built the two bricked manholes and embedded the drain system to the road connection. The mains connection to the road had to be done by the council at a suitable time. Stan of course did the foundation brickwork to floor height and I become the general labourer. It was very hard work and Stan for some reason was as keen to get on with the job as I was. He did warn me, however, that once the whole brickwork was completed I would be on my own. From this I gathered that his long-suffering family had laid down some laws and relationships were getting strained.

This was all happening during March and April in 1948 and the weather had started to improve. My first son, Peter, was born at this time. I was glad that I had worked hard at my teacher training studies during the early part of the winter and by late April I was being set tests in the form of past exam papers by Chambers College. The examinations were in early June and I was determined to do as well as I could. I knew that if I passed the more academic year one the second year of the course would be more leisurely.

It meant that I would have to spend the next year, 1949, in a secondary school as an uncertified teacher, at the same time I would have to take an examination paper on applied psychology. There were text books supplied for this and it entailed much more reading and study as the subject is so wide. In addition I had to take advanced exams in practical work and once again the taking of past papers in all of this came to my aid, when the final exams came in late 1949.

One weekend when I was working on my own another extraordinary thing happened. We had completed the brickwork footings for the foundations and my task was to fill in the floor with rubble so that a four-inch concrete floor could be put on top. The water pipe was in place for the household supply and the earthenware pipe for the toilet also in situ so we were prepared to do this connecting by hand. This, Stan and I visualised would take us several weeks of hard graft.

I was tending to this task when a large shadow formed over me and a broad Irish voice boomed out, "You're not thinking of breaking your back doing the oversite by hand, are you?" he said. I was suitably taken aback as he offered me a large hand which seemed as big as an elephant's foot. "I'll tell you what," he said, "If you get six tons of 3/8" ballast and half a ton of cement I will get my boys to do it for you for ten pounds. Have the stuff here by next Saturday and I will bring our small cement mixer, barrows and the job will be done. Ten pounds will be plenty enough for a few pints on Saturday evening," he said, "so how about that?"

I had seen this man about before and he and his gang did contract work for other builders in Chelmsford. They were as good as their word and with the minimum of fuss got this tedious and heavyweight job done for us. This meant that our first survey could take place which went successfully and I was in a position to choose the bricks and get them on order.

Stan suggested that we used soft red bricks for the face work as he had successfully used these before. I agreed. They were not long coming and came together with a suitable number of common Fletton bricks for the inside walls. We needed some special facing bricks called quoins for the corners of the bay windows and these were put to one side until needed.

Having cemented an area of damp course in place we proceeded with the walls. These were to be cavity built which meant an outer and inner wall with a space of two inches between. The walls were held together by twisted metal ties. Stan of course was familiar with this construction and my job was to mix the mortar and when able, to do some of the inner brickwork with the common flettons. These would eventually be plastered over so my brickwork didn't have to be so precise and Stan kept an eye on me by frequent visits from outside to inside to monitor my efforts.

The front and back door frames were bricked in place as we proceeded and the plan was to build up to windowsill height.

Stan would then take a few weeks off to allow me to make the window frames and get them in place. This seemed a good idea and I could make the frames and also fit my studies in at a leisurely pace. I had decided to use metal Brittall frames for the actual windows. Brittalls were a well known local firm who produced standard sized metal windows so I was able to make the surrounding wooden frame to suit these sizes. The bay windows were more difficult but as the brickwork for the bay was in place I was able to calculate the windowsills and frames and do a very good job of this.

In fact I had plenty to do as I was able to get the inside walls up to the same height as the outer walls and also put the inside door lining in place. These I made and all the woodwork was well painted with a primer coat as the frames were exposed to the elements.

This all took place in the early months of 1948 and when I took the examinations for the first year of the course I felt reasonably confident of success. These exams were at the local Technical College and took place in late June. The results were out by August and I was very relieved and pleased to have passed – no grade was given as candidates either passed or failed so it was difficult to assess how well one had done!

I now had the job of telling the firm's director that I would be leaving the firm at the end of August. I felt rather guilty as he had been good to me. I think he had in mind that I would make a decent foreman in the firm and perhaps I would have! Surprisingly he seemed pleased for me and offered his congratulations so I felt quite relieved and I left the firm quite amicably.

This type of teacher qualification meant that I would spend the second year in a secondary boys' school. This turned out to be at the local Moulsham School where I had in fact worked at erecting the type of buildings that I would do my teacher practice in. The school holiday would also be a bonus and provide valuable time on the building project so all in all 1948-49 was looking good.

Whether I had the ability to teach or not had hardly entered my mind as things had been so hectic and at times overwhelming. Anyway, I would be in at the deep end when I started in September and in truth I found myself looking forward to the challenge.

With the window and door frames in place a refreshed Stan was ready to start the last phase of the brickwork. The money situation was working out well and there was enough cement and sand on the site to finish the brickwork to the eaves level. I would then be ready to claim the final £400 with which to buy the roof materials and to pay for the internal plastering, plumbing and electrical work but that was all in the future. I also had to make the concrete lintels to go over the windows and doors. This was a relatively simple matter as I made box-like structures from old scaffold boards to the correct sizes and filled them with a suitable concrete mix. Iron rods had to be carefully placed in the concrete to add reinforcement and strength.

By the time we had the walls up to the top of the doors and windows the lintels were made and simply placed in position and bricked there. When this was completed Stan's work was done and my next job was to cement the 4" by 2" wall plates in position. These were straight pieces of good quality sawn timber and had to be jointed where necessary and embedded on top of the walls ready to take the rest of the roof structure. Another stage completed.

Stan had been as good as his word from the beginning of the venture and I realised I owed a great deal to him. He knew that I was on a very tight budget and seemed happy enough to do the work at normal rates of pay so he left me to get on with the work. He was a real friend and workmate and I will always be grateful.

The day in September came when I had to report to the school and meet Mr Hutchinson the headmaster. By a strange coincidence 1949 was to be his retirement year as he had completed forty years of service. He was very welcoming and had decided that I should be based with the junior woodwork teacher, a Mr Mardon, and after a short talk he took me along to the woodwork room and introduced me to John Mardon. He was slightly older than I was and I had no difficulty in forming a good working relationship with him and he seemed quite willing to help me and was an excellent mentor.

The setup in those days at Moulsham Secondary Modern boys' school was unusual and seemed to be in two halves – senior school and junior school. It meant that the teachers were segregated into two tiers on the whole. This didn't happen in any of the other schools I eventually taught in and I think there was resentment from the teachers who found themselves taking the eleven- and twelve-year-old pupils and then handing them on to the more established senior members of staff.

I knew that John was not happy about this and neither was his counterpart in the junior metalwork shop.

At the time to me this was just normal practice but it did mean that I spent my time in one workshop and had no opportunity to teach senior pupils.

There was another problem that I had to contend with which was quite serious for a short time. It seemed that the two senior craft teachers had spoken to the N.U.T. (National Union of Teachers) representative that my type of entry into teaching was not legitimate and they entrusted him to investigate this. Their view was that a trained teacher had to come from a teacher training or college establishment and I suppose they had a point. The NUT man in fact was quite friendly when I saw him but as he explained he just had a job to do. He said he would contact the office of the Essex Chief Education Officer and sort the matter out.

I felt a bit embarrassed by all this! After the war of course with so many teachers being lost there had been a government scheme to recruit teachers by offering a one-year emergency course. This had been accepted by the teachers' unions and many a good teacher was garnered into the profession this way.

My type of entry was by a much more rigorous scheme which entailed two years of very hard work.

It meant that intelligent craftsmen were co-opted from industrial backgrounds to fill a void. Craftwork was valued highly in schools for the whole of my thirty years of teaching. This was particularly so in the fifties and sixties when Britain was being rebuilt after a devastating war. At that time even grammar schools had workshops but I suspect these were more for leisure or hobby pursuits.

Being in the workshop with John Mardon meant that I had fallen on my feet again. He was an excellent craftsman himself and had a common sense attitude to teaching which helped me immensely. I merely observed this approach and technique for the first two weeks and then I eventually took a class for the first time while he took stock. He didn't hesitate to be kindly critical and I remember him saying to me to avoid mannerisms and being too repetitive with certain words.

He could be quite severe discipline-wise with new classes in order to stamp his authority and occasionally reverted to mild violence in order to establish this. To teach he said one had to have order and that was part of his very successful code.

Adjacent to the woodwork room was an identical metalwork room. The pupils in their first and second years at the school (11-12 years old) alternated between the two workshops. The teacher in the other workshop seemed to make very hard work of the job. He was a verbal disciplinarian and adopted a more military attitude to his pupils. This was interesting to me as an observer and part of a learning curve on my part.

Classes for woodwork were allowed to walk into the workshop, put on their aprons and stand by their allotted benches. The metalwork teacher insisted that his classes lined up outside in pairs and were absolutely quiet before they marched in. Two different ways of going about it which both worked.

As the year progressed through the winter and into spring I eventually progressed to taking a full week's classes. John was gainfully employed at the time making a loom for his wife. He was making it from a set of drawings and it turned out to be a useful work of art. It also gave him a chance to make a laminated bentwood chair that he was experimenting with.

At this time I was also taking classes in related T.D. (technical drawing) which was also very interesting. The downward side was that I was getting no experience with the senior pupils. This could have been a severe disadvantage but my industrial experience would come to my aid when I had to face this problem.

On quite a few occasions I was called upon to take classes in other subjects if staff were absent. This was good experience and did enable me to meet senior pupils. On the whole these lessons were one-off affairs and usually went quite well, in fact it seemed to me at the time that coping with more adult children could be quite rewarding.

Having more free time with holidays and light evenings I had made fair progress with the bungalow roof.

The plans of this helped a great deal and the centre part of the roof was a simple gable construction which meant that the central rafters and the ridge board was soon in position. The hip boards and spaced rafters I fitted by careful trial and error and this worked very well. Once the level cuts were established it was a careful problem of cutting and fitting.

Good progress was made as the roof began to take shape and I did the rear end first as this did not include the more complicated part over the bay window.

I didn't really rush this work and my intention was to complete the roof during the six week or so summer break starting in July.

By June I had become an accepted member of the staff at Moulsham School. The N.U.T. rep had enrolled me into the union and generally the atmosphere was friendly. He fancied himself as a DIY person and knowing of my practical ability often asked for advice. He also got me to co-opt Stan into building a brick garage for him. He did most of the woodwork himself and I found myself in an advisory capacity on the project.

It was about the beginning of June that I suddenly had a wake-up call that was to kick-start my teaching career.

I had been busy in the workshop preparing the wood which I was to use for the two advanced practical exams. These were to be held at the Technical College in Chelmsford on the last two Saturdays in June so things were already beginning to hot up.

So to be suddenly called to the headmaster's study and to be told that on the Monday following I had to report to Braintree Boys' Secondary Modern to fill in for a seriously ill woodwork teacher was quite a shock.

When I went back to the workshop to gather my bits and pieces together and tell the news to John I didn't realise that I was about to leave the school for good. I did keep well in touch with him and other staff members for many years after that and I certainly owed him a lot for his help and guidance.

Braintree is about twelve miles from Chelmsford so my faithful Norton was going to be put to good use. I remember arriving at the school on that Monday and a group of curious boys surrounding me and the machine. There was a long row of staff cars at the front of the school and it seemed that a motorcycling member of staff was a novelty. I was helpfully directed to the headmaster's office and he seemed well enough pleased to see me. He was a classical type of man more suited I thought to being a Shakespearian actor than the head of a tough school.

He took me to the workshop area and introduced me to the other two craft teachers. There was an imbalance of workshops as there were two woodwork rooms that adjoined and were part of the main building and a metalwork room that was a pre-fabricated building which stood rather isolated at the rear of the school.

The woodwork teacher whose name was Eric Goddard seemed an unassuming, easy-going man and he showed me into the room in which I would be teaching. The place was an absolute shambles! It seemed that classes had been taken by all sorts of teachers who had been required to fill in and this had resulted in chaos. After the ordered, organised teaching of John Mardon that I had got accustomed to this seemed awful and quite a shock.

Eric was quite apologetic about this and tried to be helpful. I decided to go back to the headmaster's room and requested that I had two days to get some order and time to sharpen tools and get generally organised. He surprisingly agreed and he said he would bring along a timetable of my commitments later in the day and the programme would start on the Wednesday. I took this opportunity to tell him that at the moment I was not a qualified teacher and was at the time preparing to take my final exams. He said he knew exactly what my circumstances were and that the head handicraft organiser for Essex had no doubts that I would be able to cope. This of course was a back handed compliment for me and all I had to do it seemed was to prove this confidence in me.

I was made very welcome by other members of staff and at the time treated the appointment as a temporary one which would last to the end of the term, that meant about six weeks' duration! The school was getting organised for the annual sports day. This seemed to be an important event, taken very seriously by the four school houses. As I was not a member of a house I was quickly co-opted as a judge on the day and found myself in an elevated position on the programme and hobnobbing with school governors and other elite who were performing similar duties. It seemed so funny to be so junior and yet rather important. I still have that printed programme after all those intervening years and it is a treasured memento.

The end of term came quickly enough and by this time I had completed my final exams. I felt quite confident about the two practical tests. The papers on child psychology were more difficult and I was so glad that I had read the text books thoroughly. The questions were widespread and fair and I thought my understanding of the subject would be good enough to get by.

When I left Moulsham School I was not aware than an appraisal or progress report had been required by the Ministry of Education. When I next saw John Mardon during the summer holiday session, he told me that the headmaster and himself had been required to fill in an official report on my suitability to become a teacher. It seemed that they had agreed to give me a B.1 rating which he seemed to think was very good so I had to be satisfied with that.

During the six week or so break I was able to complete the bungalow roof. I had been in contact with a tiling firm and they sent a rep along to discuss this issue. He was very helpful and gave me a price for clay roofing tiles and concrete ones. The concrete ones were considerably cheaper and I had to settle for them. When he examined the roof he suggested that I inserted more purlins at strategic places to counteract the extra weight of the concrete tiles. He said that I could save money by felting the roof and fixing the tile battens myself. This was all very helpful and I took his advice. He even gave me the exact spacing of the battens and told me how to fit the fixing pieces which gave the correct angle of the tiles at the eaves. This was essential as it married in with the correct angle for the gutter which of course had to be fitted later.

His final advice came after I had agreed terms for the job. He suggested that I contact my plumber to get the domestic hot water boiler fitted so that I could accurately fit an aperture in the roof for the chimney. Then the tilers could do the leadwork round this pipe when they did their work.

The domestic boiler system was in the form of a free-standing solid fire with an integral boiler. These were compact and provided hot water for the kitchen and bathroom. They were called 'Ideal' boilers and were finished in grey nitrous enamel and were very popular at the time.

While working for 'Selwoods', the building firm, I had got to know various tradesmen and had no difficulty in getting a plumber. He came and gave me a price for doing the whole job and while putting in the boiler and its flue he was able to measure and get the job organised, to complete when the inside of the bungalow got to that stage.

As the six week school holiday neared its end I had got the roof ready for tiling. The contractor came to ensure that everything was in order and a few days later the tiles and men arrived. They worked amazingly quickly and took less than a day to complete the whole roof. I suppose to them a small bungalow would have been a simple task but it was obvious to me that their skill and teamwork was paramount.

Another thing that happened about this time was that on getting to the in-laws home one evening there was a letter from the Essex Education Authority. This simply stated that tragically the teacher whose place I had been temporarily filling at Braintree had died. They required that I return to the school in September to continue as a temporary stand-in. I knew that my final examination results would not be out until later on, probably October, so I was pleased enough to return.

When September came the internal work or finishing was the main work to be done. I had made arrangements with an electrician to do the wiring at his leisure. I knew him well as he was a fellow motorcyclist and used a sidecar as his workhorse. He did the job at a very competitive price; he said he had been able to use plugs, switches and cable left over from other jobs. Once the electrical work had been done the plastering and plumbing were the main things to be completed.

Having to start teaching in earnest in September I had decided to let the bungalow work become more leisurely during that winter term as I needed to concentrate on my new career. I did, however, hope that I could begin to decorate the rooms during the Christmas break. I knew that the flooring which would be in the form of Marley tiles would best be laid after the decorating. This eventually worked out well and the whole floor was laid by a specialist firm. Marley tiles of course were inclined to be a cold type of flooring but by far the cheapest in those days. They could be had in various colours and were cemented into place, the 'layers' were expert at fitting the tiles into awkward places and the final work was very satisfactory.

On my return to the school at Braintree I was made very welcome, especially by the senior staff members. I was given a full workload from the off and found myself teaching at all age levels. The school leaving age at this time was fourteen, this meant that if a pupil became fourteen during the winter term he could leave at Christmas, this of course also applied to the spring term.

Therefore, taking senior classes had the bonus of being reduced as the year progressed. There were no external examinations at that time and much more emphasis was put on gainful employment so that practical subjects were held in quite high esteem.

From my army days I had learnt to play Bridge and had always been a keen card player. The senior staff members had two Bridge school games going during lunch break and I was frequently able to fill in if someone was absent. This I found rather embarrassing as being new to the job I had plenty to do in my workshop and was still in the process of establishing myself in my work. However, the school itself was run smoothly and efficiently by these senior teachers as the headmaster seemed to be more of a figurehead so I found it difficult to refuse to play. I certainly enjoyed playing Bridge and I still do so I had to compromise to some extent.

Since I was still a temporary member of staff I had not been asked to join a school house. Being neutral, so to speak, I found myself in great demand as a referee for the house football matches, especially the senior ones.

These were taken very seriously and needed careful handling. I knew the rules fairly well as I had played for an army team during the war. The boys seemed to sense that I tried to do a fair job and all this tended to help my standing as a teacher in the school.

When in late October I had the notification that I had got my teaching certificate no-one at the school seemed surprised, they merely said that they would have been very taken aback if I had not got it. Because of the kindness and help of John Mardon and the headmaster at Moulsham I had in fact achieved a first class pass and it was nice to think that the hard work had paid off.

When I informed the headmaster at Braintree he merely said that he was applying for me to have a permanent post at the school. It seemed at the time I had little choice in the matter and in fact I considered myself quite lucky as the school had a happy atmosphere and I felt quite at home.

In those days one's salary was tied to the Burnham scale and a teacher new to the work got a salary of one increment a year increase for the first fourteen years. This meant that a young teacher straight from college would be fourteen years before getting maximum salary. I am not sure that this applies to new teachers in today's educational climate but it was the norm then.

When I received from Essex Education my official appointment to Braintree Boys' Secondary Modern School I had quite a pleasant surprise. They had given me four increments for industrial service and five more for war service and were counting my probationary year at Moulsham as a further one year increment. This was very good news of course and at the ripe old age of 29 years old I could hope to be on maximum teachers' pay in four years.

The headmaster at the school was a Mr Freeman who seemed to me to be a scholarly person. He and one of the senior English teachers were very keen on school drama productions. During 1950 they were planning to do a Gilbert and Sullivan light opera of H.M.S. Pinafore. This eventually took place and was a great success. The boys chosen to do the feminine parts did exceedingly well and the overall performances were excellent. Both woodwork shops were employed with making props and the whole school had an enjoyable time. I remember taking Peter to see one of the shows and it had quite a marked effect on him.

That first year for me went quite quickly. By the end of it we had moved into our new home. I had changed the Norton for a smaller bike, a BSA Bantam. This was my first new machine ever and was lighter to ride and very economical to run. The early months of 1951 were not good from a weather point of view. I can remember riding that bike to work in conditions bad enough to stop buses and other forms of transport from moving. I tended to ride along near the verge or gutter and this helped me to control the bike on the slippery surface.

By this time my son Peter was approaching his third year and our second child was due in February 1950. It was another boy and he was named David and our future looked very set and good. Looking back over the last five years it had certainly been a busy period with a capital B.

From Thirty to Thirty-Five

As May approached and with it my thirtieth birthday a fairly mundane era unfolded.

My work was proceeding to plan. I was by now a house member of staff but these duties were not too onerous. The houses had colours and I found myself in grey house, the head of house whose name was Youngman was an established senior teacher and ran things very efficiently. I helped with the sports coaching and was required to take some house assemblies. These had a religious bias in those days and I found myself in a little trouble on one occasion. Because practical subjects were usually popular I got on quite well with the senior boys. One of my classes was 4D and they were a small group who were rather academically retarded. I had got them interested in a garden project and this included making a wheelbarrow and trug baskets, handles for tools and even making garden labels.

When I was to take my next assembly I tried to persuade five of the boys of 4D to do a reading. This I knew would be a risky challenge for them and for me. Without thinking too much about it I took along my favourite copy of A.E. Houseman's 'A Shropshire Lad' and we selected a reading for each boy and five of the boys agreed to do it. When the Monday came to begin our assembly I had not told anyone about my intentions and when I arrived on stage with my five volunteers this caused a bit of a stir. The Houseman poems in the main are about war and games or sport and I had no qualms about their suitability.

I did a short introductory assembly talk and then introduced each lad who in fact did their individual reading quite well and seemed quite pleased with themselves.

When the assembly was over Mr Youngman accosted me as I was leaving the stage. He said, "You did that on purpose, didn't you". I just said I didn't understand what he meant, and he said, "You knew damned well that Houseman was a leading atheist of his time". This in fact was not true, as I didn't know that. He then congratulated me for getting the lads of 4D to perform so well so it all ended smoothly.

The form teacher for that year's 4D was a matronly lady called Mrs. Maidment. She was a very good remedial teacher with a firm motherly approach and these rather awkward and sometimes difficult fourteen-year-old boys had a great deal of respect for her.

I was also fortunate during that first year at Braintree to have 4A for woodwork. Eric Goddard had 4B and 4C at this time and when the next year came this was to be reversed which was fair and good.

Streaming to my idea in those days worked very well and I could never understand why in later years in secondary education it would be abandoned for mixed ability grouping.

The "A" stream class in 1950 seemed to be a bright, happy bunch of lads. Some of them had been 11+ failures, they however found themselves in the top echelons of the Secondary Modern School whereas some of their contemporaries at the local grammar school were unhappy at being in lower classes.

They certainly worked very hard at their academic lessons and were also keen at sport and craftwork. During that first term I had been asked by a Mr Ing who ran the youth centre if I would do an evening class in woodwork. When I accepted I found that the nucleus of the class were from 4A, and in that way the work they were doing in lessons during the day could be continued with during the evenings. They were able to make very useful pieces of furniture and enjoyed doing it. The local newspaper did an article on the youth centre and its activities and this included a photograph of some of the students and myself in the workshop. I still have that photograph among my souvenirs.

One of the keener lads was involved in the H.M.S. Pinafore production and was taking the part of Buttercup. He had to take a fair bit of ribbing from his mates but took it all in good part.

The teacher in charge of drama was a Mr Moll and when I first saw him I knew that I had encountered him before. He was an eccentric type of person who tended to stand out in a crowd.

When I was stationed at Beirut he had been one of the RAF office corporals at 241 Wing and many times had signed for dispatches that I had delivered. He had no inkling of who I was of course, just another scruffy dispatch rider among many! He in those days tended to have longer hair than we were permitted, and he looked rather ungainly in his khaki drill uniform with longer than usual shorts. Somehow, he just looked what he really was – a square peg in a round hole. His Christian name was Victor and both the teachers and pupils called him Victor Hugo. He didn't seem to mind. He was in fact very good at his job and a cheerful and pleasant colleague when you got to know him.

Those first two years at the school went quickly and very well for me. The headmaster Mr Freeman had left by this time and had been replaced by a Mr A Gregson who was a tougher character and I thought ideal for the job. He was going to be important as well in my later career and seemed to be a man with aims and the determination to put them into practice.

Our small family was also flourishing well and the boys Peter and David seemed to be healthy and quite bright. I remember taking Joyce and Peter to a classical concert at the Odeon Cinema in Chelmsford, the programme included Dvorak's New World Symphony and Peter really seemed to enjoy that at the age of five or thereabouts. He also seemed to be interested in castles and it is time to say that music, and history, have been important to him throughout his life. He was very much a studious child and read a lot. I remember he had the habit of getting a virgin piece of paper on the table and taking ages in deciding what to put on it, sometimes a drawing or sometimes a piece of prose. He seemed to have little interest in games or sport and that was the way he was and still is.

David at two years or so seemed to be developing a more adventurous role and even at that age was showing an aptitude for figures. Maths would turn out to be his forte and he would eventually get a degree in Maths at Cambridge.

Peter, I think, was destined to teach and got his necessary qualifications at Exeter University, he always seemed happy at this vocation and became very good at it.

All of this of course was in the future and many good as well as bad things were to happen in the years between.

In early 1952 I had a letter from one of the teachers who was at Moulsham School when I was there. He was quite elderly and had since retired from his senior maths position at the school and his name was Mr Smith. In the letter he asked me if I could possibly do some woodwork repairs for him to his house and as he lived fairly near to us I went along to see him.

He needed a new gate and repairs to his garage doors, and one or two jobs doing inside the house. When examining the garage doors I noticed that he had a vehicle in the garage that was covered in old sheets, with cardboard boxes full of odds and ends on top of its roof. The wheels were showing below and it was resting on flat tyres and when I enquired about it he said that he had driven pre-war and it had been covered up since 1939 when petrol rationing had started. The car turned out to be an Austin Seven saloon of 1931 vintage and when I ran my finger along one of the doors it revealed a shiny blue surface underneath. When I asked him for more details he said that the engine had been re-bored about 1938 and we thought the car could be put into working order. Being elderly he was not going to drive any more, he said, so I asked him if he would sell it to me. We came to terms for the vehicle and he said if I would complete the work and give him forty pounds I could have it and so that came about.

Our next door neighbour who was named Mr Baker was quite a friendly person who was knowledgeable about motor cars so when I had completed the jobs at Mr Smith's we went along to have a closer look at the car. It seemed in good condition for its age and with new tyres fitted we were able to tow it back to Wallace Crescent for further mechanical inspection. After fitting a new battery we were able to get it running well and it turned out to be quite a bargain.

Although I had passed army tests to drive four wheel vehicles I had not had the foresight to convert my service licence to a civilian one so I was faced with passing the appropriate driving test. My associate teaching friend Eric Goddard who drove a more modern Austin Ruby saloon kindly agreed to teach me how to drive his vehicle. It was more a question of getting used to driving a car than anything else and after a few weeks' experience I was ready to take the test. The test was held in Chelmsford and I was able to practice on the route to some extent but on the day of the test I almost blew it. When I set off with this route in mind I didn't listen to his initial instructions and took a first right instead of a left. He made me stop and I remember him saying, "For the purposes of getting you to the testing area will you please listen to my instructions".

Well, I thought this would mean failure so I tended, I suppose, to relax more and managed to get round the rest of the course quite well. When he gave me a pass certificate I was pleased and very relieved to have got through the ordeal.

So in early 1952 I sold my BSA motorcycle and became a more staid family man driver. I did have to spend more money on the car but it served for quite a few years and was certainly value for money. I never regretted my motorcycle days and still followed motorcycle sporting events. On several occasions, when visiting my brother Leslie in Northern Ireland we went to race meetings such as the Ulster Grand Prix and the North West 200. By this time in the late fifties and sixties the races were being dominated by Italian or Japanese machines. The British motorcycle industry seemed just to fade away after the second world war and has never recovered, which to me seems a very depressing situation.

Another thing that shortened my motorcycling career also happened in early 1950. The weather was very frosty and foggy and getting to school and back had been difficult that day. When I got home to Chelmsford there was a note from my stepfather saying that Mother was unwell. At the time my parents were living in Danbury which is about five miles from Chelmsford. By now they were both quite elderly although my stepfather was still working and had in fact a job with the council working on the roads which again was unfamiliar territory to him.

Self, age 16 years

Leslie, age 25 years

Gordon, 1941

Sister Doreen and son Mick, 1941

SHQ Team RAF, February 1943

Fred mending a puncture in the Sinai Desert, May 1942

Hommes Road near Affise, Syria, March 1943

With Sticky and Jock, Aleppo, Syria, February 1943

British Embassy, Cairo 1944

Simba and self in Embassy
Ground, Cairo, September 1945

Peter on B.S.A Bantam, 1950

Teaching at first school, Braintree, Essex, 1952

With Peter and David, 1953

First car with David, 1955

The Heath Bentwaters Suffolk, 1955. We lived in
the right hand dwelling.

Peter and David, Christ's
Hospital, 1963

Mother and Stepfather Perce, 1960

Jo as a nurse, 1950

Junior Cricket team, Hedley Walter School, 1966

All the boys together, holiday at Pwllheli, 1965
Left to right: David, Matt, Simon, Tim, Peter

Tim and Matt at a festival, 1976

From left to right: Gordon, Leslie and Ken, 1989

After ten that day I set off still in the inclement weather to see if I could be of any help. It appeared that Mum had been dozing off during the afternoon and had toppled sideways onto the open coal fire and had burnt her face rather badly, including her ear. My rather stupid stepfather had not informed, let alone taken her to the doctor, so I had to sort that out before returning home to Wallace Crescent.

During the evening I had the onset of a terrible pain in my chest. I was having difficulty breathing and my wife had no option but to get a doctor out. I can still remember the severity of that attack and from that day to this I have never experienced such agony. When the pain subsided to some extent and the doctor had examined me he declared that I would have to rest for three weeks. I was subjected to several tests at the local hospital including an electro-cardiograph examination.

The pain never returned again and I was allowed to return to teaching. For many years after that I was really worried that this could happen again as it had been a sobering experience. Now, so many years afterwards I have come to the conclusion that it was brought about by the stresses of that one day!

By this time my mother was recovering from her burns, she was certainly a tough lady and merely shrugged off her problems and grew her hair longer to cover her disfigured ear.

By this time I was organised with the car and it was performing well. We had in fact family transport which was good. The car itself was an old vehicle and showed it. By the 1950s saloon cars of modern vintage had become quite smart. But we were happy enough just to be mobile and my school journeys were much better. The car had no heating of course and the windscreen wipers had to be worked manually but I managed, and felt lucky to have four safe wheels.

It was about this time I decided to take a craft examination in metalwork, so I contacted Chambers College in Kent and started the necessary studies. This to some extent had been prompted by John Mardon. He had started to do a metalwork course at the Chelmsford Technical College for one evening a week so I joined him in order to get more practical experience. The course turned out to be orientated towards beaten metalwork which meant working in copper, brass and silver plate. It was very interesting and I learnt a lot especially in the use of heat treatment, silver soldering and the many uses of the blowtorch. Towards the end of the course I had enough all-round practical knowledge to pass the exam. This in later years helped to further my career when I was looking for advancement.

Joyce, my wife, had a favourite friend during these years and her name was Kathy Brennan, and she was one of four daughters. The family were very religious and were of the Catholic faith and we came to know them all very well. Kathy would have been about twenty years old at the time and her two elder sisters had gone from the local Catholic school on to university and had eventually married. The younger sister Marie was about fourteen at the time and was developing into a beautiful young lady. I remember pulling her leg about breaking all the boys' hearts and her parents chiding me for spoiling her with my remarks.

Jo, who was my wife's cousin often came to visit us, she was the daughter of Joyce's father's sister so was a first cousin. She was very fond of Peter and David and tended to spoil them at times and she and our family sometimes went out together on outings and picnics.

Sometime during 1953 Kathy became engaged and soon announced her marriage. She had become very close to Joyce and Kathy said they were moving to some place in the Midlands called Todmorden after the wedding. I think Joyce was quite disappointed. It all happened quite quickly and the two women kept in touch by letters after that.

My first four years as a teacher at Braintree went steadily along but towards the end of 1953 an event happened that was to turn our lives around. On arriving home from school I was met at the door by the district nurse who told me that during the afternoon Joyce had phoned her to say she was unwell which turned out to be no exaggeration. She was very poorly indeed and when the doctor came she was soon on her way to the local isolation hospital. By the time I had got home she was in fact paralysed from the neck down and fighting for her life in an iron lung. She had contracted poliomyelitis in its most virulent form. This disease in this country was said to be a thing of the past and apparently the epidemic that brought about her condition was the last to have such a devastating effect in the land. The saddest thing was that because her lungs were so badly affected that it was not possible to give her any physiotherapy as she could not be taken out of the breathing apparatus for more than a few moments at a time.

We, that is Peter, David and myself were placed in isolation for three weeks and confined to the bungalow. The district nurse was a friendly acquaintance as I had met her before when sister Doreen had had her second child, Rosalind. In fact I had speedily been sent to get the nurse when the baby had been due. She, the nurse, was in fact in attendance each day seeing to our needs and supplies and also to make sure that we had none of the polio symptoms.

At the end of the three weeks I had some problems to resolve. I had a committed job to consider in the first case. Sister Doreen, bless her, was quite willing to look after David. He was a quiet little boy of three and a half years and not yet at school so that arrangement was fine. My mother who was well into her sixties agreed to have Peter and he attended a junior school in Danbury.

After about a month in the local isolation hospital, Joyce was moved to a specialist unit at Rush Green near Romford which was about twelve miles from Chelmsford. Joyce's mother and father who were approaching their seventies were also very helpful but they had no transport of their own and had to rely on buses to get about. It was not easy for them to get to Rush Green as they had to change buses at Romford. Occasionally they took the boys to see their mother at Rush Green but it was not easy for them.

From time to time during visits to see Joyce I was called to the hospital office and given an assessment on her condition and they could offer no hope about her condition changing. The outlook indeed looked very bleak; in fact the next years gradually became intolerable. I was travelling twelve miles one way to school, keeping contact with the boys and having to travel to the hospital in the other direction.

I don't remember feeling sorry for myself about this but life was beginning to be really hard physically. On occasions I had met Jo, Joyce's cousin, while visiting the hospital and we gradually formed an attachment. Sometimes we went to a cinema or concert together and then we started a serious affair. We both felt quite guilty about this as we both held responsible positions in life but it happened. When I think back on all this I just feel that in similar circumstances we would have to do the same again.

It all seemed very unfair all round, I was particularly concerned about my ageing mother having to cope during the week with Peter. David seemed happy with Doreen and her husband Dennis but having had their own children it seemed rather unfair on them especially as there seemed no end in sight.

Towards the end of that school year I wrote to the Education Authority in Essex stating that due to family difficulties I was leaving teaching that July and getting a job in Chelmsford more central to home. They replied immediately that if I would take a temporary craft teaching job in Harold Hill which is near Romford in September that I would be given the woodwork post at the new Broomfield school in Chelmsford when it opened after the Christmas holidays. They said they were aware of my difficulties and would indeed be very disappointed if I left teaching.

All this did eventually come about and I was destined to spend five good years at the Broomfield school.

I was very sad to leave the school at Braintree. The headmaster, Mr Gregson, gave me a good reference when I left and his next statement rather surprised me. He assured me that in the future he was to be the designated headmaster of the first comprehensive school in Essex and it would be at Brentwood. He also said that if I kept an eye out in the 'Times Educational Supplement' and applied for a job at the school he would look upon such an appointment favourably and it would be a post with special responsibility. This did all come to pass and considering it happened five years later this was all very remarkable.

As I am writing this, at quite a considerable age, my thoughts often return to certain past parts of my life. I have not been a religious person even though my twin sister and I were made to go to church regularly every Sunday. We were choir members and also had to attend Sunday school. I am sure that we resented the fact that the other members of the family rarely went near the church except on specific occasions.

However, I have always respected other people's leaning towards their beliefs and even been a little envious of their certainty in their various Gods. There being various and so many multiple beliefs could be the reason why I find it difficult to comprehend religion. There is only one thing certain and that is in the near future I will find out, or not, about these things. I realised that I will have some explaining to do to God if there is one about some aspects of my actions in life. My first wife would be keen to get some answers I am sure. The fact that I severely injured an Arab whilst being on duty as a dispatch rider during the Second World War would also be an answerable discredit. That is on my conscience despite the fact that we had direct orders from the army that in no circumstances were we to stop if such an incident occurred. Getting our no doubt important dispatches delivered was our priority always and there was a war to be won.

The period of my life between the ages of thirty and thirty-five are somewhat blurred. It was a hellish time! I suppose it must have been about 1954 when my liaison with Jo was about a year old that we decided to part. By this time Jo was a staff nurse and had a job in the General Hospital in Romford. I suppose we were both suffering some pangs of conscience and we were certain that Joyce was aware of the situation as Jo no longer felt able to visit her in hospital. We occasionally spent time together at weekends at the bungalow in Wallace Crescent and were aware of strange looks from neighbours although no one said anything. I remember the weekend that we reluctantly parted as when I went to bed that night my nursing acquaintance had made me an apple pie bed. This meant that the sheets were fitted to the bed in such a way that a person couldn't get into it. This was of course a sort of impish joke and I had to fully unmake the bed and remake it before I could use it.

The following weeks were pretty miserable for me. I know that Jo's parents were pleased that some sort of rift had taken place. They lived in a nice part of Harold Wood near Romford. I remember them often saying to Jo that they hoped he wouldn't park that disreputable old car too near their property as there had been occasions when it had embarrassed them.

In the meantime things had not improved for Joyce and for the most part her existence in a horrible coffin-like open-ended iron lung had not improved. There were short durations when she was taken from the lung and connected to another breathing device that was more portable. It had a very noisy bellows attachment but it did mean that she was out of an enclosure for short periods.

Strangely enough it was this change of circumstances that brought matters to a head. Mostly when I visited at weekends I had Peter and David with me. They would talk to their mother for a while and then there was little for them to do so our visits were reluctantly short.

One weekend when I arrived Joyce was attached to this other machine and she made a statement quite out of the blue which astounded me. She said wouldn't it be possible for her to come home using this apparatus and that Jo and myself could be the nursing support for her, or words to that effect. I remember being taken aback by this improbable suggestion. It did suggest to me however that Joyce somehow in her own mind was beginning to realise that Peter and David needed a home life which she could no longer give them.

Of course when I took this idea up with the medical staff they assured me that if this was even remotely practical that Joyce in an ordinary environment would get pneumonia with fatal results.

It was about two weeks later on a Sunday that I made a decision. I was feeling pretty miserable and somewhat desperate at the time. I was faced with my normal programme: first to Danbury to pick up Peter then to Doreen's to collect David and then on to Rush Green.

When I arrived at Mother's I made a declaration that I intended to sell the bungalow and buy an old property to live in and renovate. I was going to ask Jo to live with me and start a new existence.

Quite to my amazement my mother said, "Why has it taken so long to come to this decision?" She pointed out obvious advantages and that everyone was entitled to some form of life and it was high time that I did something about it.

That day when I collected David I chickened out of telling sister Doreen of my intentions. Over the years she had been very helpful and good to me. She and husband Dennis had lived a fairly sedentary life and altogether things had gone well for them. She was not a religious person as such but she was rather prudish and straight-laced. She was often in contact with Mother at Danbury so I thought I would let the grapevine syndrome work and of course it did. She certainly gave me her candid opinion when I next saw her; fortunately she had in the meantime been talking to my friendly district nurse. The nurse had pointed out the hopelessness of my position and even went as far as saying it was a pity that Joyce had survived the initial disease, as her quality of life was so poor.

In the meantime I scoured the local paper for suitably priced properties and decided to visit South Woodham Ferrers to view three that looked promising. One of these was actually in North Woodham and stood in a fork of two roads in the village quite close to the church. When I had viewed the other places in South Woodham I realised that the most suitable one was the North Woodham property and I returned to give this a second perusal. The problem was that it was in quite a busy street, parking would be difficult and not too safe for children.

The most suitable one of the two in South Woodham was about a hundred yards down an unmade road. The house was called "Avenue Villa" and it was on Mount Pleasant Road. It had water and electricity laid on and was lockable and more or less habitable. A great deal of renovating needed doing, which I could see would involve underpinning the two front corners of the house. The house itself was a simple structure with two good size rooms downstairs with bedrooms above and at the back was a kitchen and above that a smaller bedroom. The staircase went up between the rooms from a small hall inside the front door and there was an open porch outside which gave some shelter.

Having made the decision things happened quite quickly. The bungalow at Wallace Crescent sold within a day or two of advertising it. I had priced it at £2,250 and an anxious buyer put a £250 deposit on it almost immediately. Paying off the outstanding amount to the Salvation Army Insurance Company proved to be a simple matter and after the bungalow sale and the following negotiations, I ended up with £900.

The asking sum for the old house at South Woodham was £850 and to settle a deal for this I had to go to the small town of Wickford, Essex. The firm of solicitors was based in the high street and over the ensuing years we were to use their services on quite a few occasions.

Precise dates are not clear to me during this period. We probably moved into Avenue Villa about June 1954, I know I left the Braintree school at the end of the school year which was July of that year.

There was a local removal firm in the village and I made arrangements with them for the move. Jo and I travelled in the Austin, picking up David and then Peter from Mother's bungalow in Danbury. For better or for worse we were making a fresh start. The boys, I remember, soon settled in at the local (primary infants) school. Living in the old house was hard at first but our all round efforts to improve our life soon began to pay dividends.

In September I took up the temporary job at Harold Hill in West Essex. Teaching there proved to be quite an eye-opener. It was a London overflow school and had a tough reputation, the main sport there was boxing and the school had a large gymnasium geared to this activity. I found that generally the pupils were easy to get on with if certain allowances were made; there were hard cases as many were from tough backgrounds and broken homes. They seemed to have a cockney type of humour and even a heart of gold under that toughness.

The job itself was routine enough, the post had been advertised without much success and even with the sweetener of a Grade 1 post there had been no takers. I was quite glad when eventually I was relieved as my journey from South Woodham to Harold Hill was over twenty miles and meant negotiating the busy Southend-on-Sea arterial road (A12) which even in the Fifties was quite hazardous.

At about half term of that 1954 winter term I found myself filling in at the other Chelmsford Secondary Modern School. I centred myself in the workshop area but spent most of that six weeks or so covering for absent teachers. I was due to go to the Broomfield School in the New Year and the short sojourn at Rainsford was useful experience. I found myself taking quite a few games lessons and one of the fourteen-year-old pupils was Geoff Hurst who was to become famous during the 1966 World Cup success.

The woodwork teacher at Rainsford, I think his name was Witten, was a keen motorcyclist and had several vintage bikes that he raced. My stay at both Harold Hill and Rainsford schools was good in some ways and gave me an insight into the large differences there are between different areas and types of pupils.

The school at Broomfield was spanking new, being on the outskirts of Chelmsford it catered for a mixed bag of pupils and was co-educational. This was a new experience and a very pleasant one. The headmaster was a Mr Eden and turned out to be very efficient but a little stuffy at times. At least he allowed his staff to get on with their work and I was to enjoy my four year stay there. My co-craft teacher who taught in the metalwork shop was named Ted Phillips. It seemed that although he was a qualified craft teacher, he had for many years been teaching in junior schools. He was a large, bluff kind of person with a rather dominating personality but somehow the pupils and staff took to him. We got on quite well as a department. He had a young daughter, who seemed to live with a mother who was married to someone else. He often had the child at weekends and was obviously very fond of her. They sometimes came to visit us at Avenue Villa and spent a pleasant few hours with us.

My first year at Broomfield Secondary Modern went quite smoothly. Although it had been up and running for about six months, the headmaster told us that there was to be an official opening on a certain date. This was to be done by R.A.B. Butler who I suppose at the time was the Tory minister for education. Understandably, the headmaster became rather worried and flustered about all this and also determined that everything would go well on the day. Ted Phillips and I were summoned to his office and told rather than asked that we get one of our more talented boys to make a suitable craft object to present to the minister on the day. This for me was not too difficult a task as one or two of the boys had become quite proficient on the woodwork lathe. We decided on a chunky type of table lamp and as the material was to hand we used mahogany. Everything went well and the lamp was wax finished and the dark brown wood looked very nice. I was given money from the school petty cash to buy the electrical fittings and a suitable shade. This was where things went slightly wrong and I lost favour at least temporarily with our headmaster.

With the wood being a dark reddy brown I chose a nicely shaped red shade and when fitted up the whole lamp looked very good.

In the meantime Ted was struggling with the metalwork object. He had chosen a fairly large copper dish and one of his boys had successfully cut out the shape and decorated the edges and beaten the blank to a suitable shape. To get a good finish on the surface with a planishing hammer was proving very difficult for the boy to do. In all honesty it is a process that can only be successfully done by an experienced silversmith. With only a short time to go the whole procedure had to be repeated and Ted himself put the finishing touches to the dish.

The day before the big event the head came to my workshop to pick up the lamp. His first remarks were, "Why have you done that, it won't do you know". He was of course referring to the colour of the shade. He may have been aware of my socialist views but I still couldn't believe that he wanted me to change the shade for a new one.

Nevertheless I had to go back to the shop in Chelmsford and change the damned thing and even today I cannot believe that anyone could be so biased. I felt like boycotting the whole ceremony, but in the end I had to apply common sense.

All seemed to be well on the day and the niceties prevailed.

At least R.A.B. had to put up with a school dinner but even that seemed to have been guaranteed and certainly better than we had on most days.

From Thirty-Five to Forty

As my thirty-fifth year approached life had begun to take some sort of pattern again. My first task in the old house was to get the kitchen organised. This entailed taking out the old oven-type range, removing the old under fire type of copper and also taking out the old flagstone floor. One couldn't help but make progress as the whole place was badly run down. I think that the way that Jo took to all this rugged domesticity was remarkable. She of course was used to hard work and she had been and still was a nurse of the old school. It really was hard graft for both of us and I think we tended to bury ourselves in sheer effort.

I had to dig out the kitchen floor and level it before concreting it. There was a builders' merchant in the village and during the coming years I became one of his best customers. He could supply most of the materials I needed and he would deliver if necessary. We laid the floor with quarry tiles and grouted cement between them. Fitting a sink and an electric water heater ensured a hot water supply and with the cold supply in place we made good progress. That sink which was fairly large was to be our children's bath and our up and down type of wash for the next ten years or so. We just got used to it and as we had electricity we were able to install a twin tub washing machine and also had an electric cooker in place.

In the meantime I had the job of taking Peter and David to Joyce's parents in Chelmsford. This occurred twice a month and sometimes more and they took the boys to see their mother on these occasions. This was usually on a Saturday and they did their travelling by bus. I suppose the boys got rather spoiled on these occasions which was to be expected. Both Peter and David were prone to travel sickness and as they were often over-indulged with cakes or sweets on these occasions this could have disastrous results on the journey home.

I suppose it was at about this time that Jo become pregnant with our son Simon. This fact when known seemed to prompt Joyce to consider divorce proceedings.

In spite of the circumstances and problems Joyce's mother and father never made life difficult for me and I thought that was to their great credit.

Of course I had to go to some London offices for the divorce hearing and surprisingly the judge turned out to be a well known figure of law.

The case itself, to my surprise, lasted only a few minutes, he merely stated that sadly the marriage could have no future and the decree was therefore granted.

Where the main Hullbridge Road and Mount Pleasant Road intersected there stood another house that was identical to Avenue Villa. The owner was a gents' hairdresser who at the time had a business in Southend-on-Sea. I think he also owned an old car to travel to work as he would have had about ten or eleven miles to get there. His name was Bert Kilden and he had his wife Sylvia lived at this house with two young daughters, Marylin and Barbara. We got to know them very well over the years; he was a DIY enthusiast and always seemed to be working on the house as we were, and the children were all at school together in the village.

They, I remember, also had the attraction of a television set, black and white of course. I knew that Peter and David went there to see children's programmes and I can remember seeing cup final events on one or two occasions.

Sylvia worked at Wickford and for many years she travelled to work with me as Wickford was on my route to school. Travelling from South Woodham presented me with a timing problem that lasted all the years we lived there.

The South Woodham railway station crossed the road almost in the centre of the village and it had manned level crossing gates. The station was on the main route from Southminster to London via Shenfield. This track from Wickford to Southminster was single track and this meant that trains often had to be sidetracked at South Woodham for trains to pass one another.

We unfortunately lived on the wrong side of this crossing and if I left my journey too late I would easily get delayed by fifteen minutes or more which meant that I would be late for school. So it was necessary to leave home at 7:15am on each school day. I soon got used to this and the fact that I was arriving at school soon after 8:00am gave me an opportunity to get my day started well. To compensate for this I endeavoured to leave school soon after 4:00pm without too much loss of conscientiousness but of course this was often not possible as I had a senior position to consider.

Starting that early meant that passenger Sylvia was getting to her job too early in Wickford but she didn't seem to mind.

During the winter of 1955 I began to get minor but irritating problems with the little car. I had about a hundred yards of unmade track to negotiate from the main road to the house. The road was also used by farm traffic and this was in some ways a bad thing and in others my salvation.

One of these tractor drivers lived further up Mount Pleasant Road and he seemed to use the tractor as transport. Over these early years he towed me out of trouble on numerous occasions, the Austin being small was easy to tow. He took this duty as a matter of course and with a smile, as it is true to say that the state of the track was down to the heavy farm traffic and he seemed to realise that.

The little car had given me over forty thousand miles of relatively free trouble when I decided to change it. A fellow teacher from another Chelmsford school had shown an interest in the car and I sold it to him for the same sum that I paid for it - £40.

With my building projects in mind I decided that some form of utility vehicle was what I needed so I bought a new Morris Minor van. It was permissible to fit side windows into vans in those days. It was a question of cutting the panels accurately and buying the safety glass. You could buy grooved rubber strip specially made for the job to complete this and so it was done. I obtained a back seat without much trouble and bolted this to the van floor with large wing nuts as fasteners. This allowed me to have a new car-cum-van which did a dual job excellently.

The Morris Minor engine in that van was very easy to maintain. The car version became legendary and many examples have been restored and can be seen today. It was a nice feeling to have a reliable form of transport. I did the maintenance on the car myself. The wheel bearings and break cables, and suspension were all fitted with grease nipples, I believe there were about fourteen altogether on the vehicle so regular attention to this was required.

The pupils at the school in the main were a joy to teach. Some of the less able boys could be troublesome and I found in all my teaching years in craftwork that good organisation paid off. This meant that I could cope with any contingency. I often did garden projects with less able pupils. A wooden wheelbarrow was a good central project and three or more boys would work on this together and it was something interesting. It was possible to buy a suitable wheel and axle with a pneumatic tyre. This then was a starting point and encouragement to get the project started. Other lads in the class made various tool handles, trug buckets and even simple seed tables as part of the scheme. This was also educationally sound as it meant correlation between departments and this went down well with the headmaster.

Materials supplied to schools such as woods and metals came through what was known as County Supplies. This was all contracted and priced very reasonably. In our departments we were given a budget for each year and I was able to get quite good quality softwoods as well as some choice of hardwoods. There was a semi-hardwood called Semba that was very popular because it was straight grained and free from knots. This was ideal as it took a good finish. The oak and mahogany on offer were usually equatorial substitutes that often varied considerably in quality and were slightly more expensive. I was also able to sometimes get offcuts from various timber merchants and these were very useful for turned work. Occasionally local builders would give to the school and in this way stocks could be kept quite healthy.

Pupils were also expected to pay a nominal sum for their completed work. Any such remuneration could be got back after the money had been garnered and gone through the office. This meant that a special duplicated book was used to enter this money in, and the cash had to be checked by one of the secretaries.

Over the years more able senior pupils did some very good work in the design and making of furniture. Their skills developed as they progressed through the school from their first year up to their fourth. The leaving age was still fourteen and that was the norm at the time.

Many pupils at Broomfield came in from various villages. Getting them to school was the parents' responsibility as there were no special buses laid on. Many children cycled to school, others walked and I suppose some were lifted in by parents with cars.

On one occasion when one of the senior pupils had completed a fairly large writing desk in oak, he was having difficulties in transporting it home. In a moment of weakness I said I could help out by using my Morris to take it home for him. We loaded it on and he directed me to this farm cottage where he lived. This turned out to be down many muddy country lanes and not at all a nice journey. It did seem worthwhile, as his mum was so grateful and pleased that the boy had made such a nice object and her smile itself was worth the effort.

By 1959 the school had increased its pupil numbers and had become a four form entry. This meant that the intake for that year had been about 144 children, four classes or forms of about 36 children in each. A notice went up that various members of staff had been awarded Grade 1 posts for special responsibility and the post for craft had gone to my colleague Ted Phillips. I don't remember being too upset by this but I had by then been teaching craftwork for almost ten years and decided to keep my eye open for another job which offered advancement. It was really a question of taking the 'Times Educational Supplement' on a regular basis and this I did.

Within a week or two, and as if by magic, there appeared in the advertisements some posts for the coming comprehensive at Brentwood. This was to be the school that the headmaster from Braintree had mentioned when I left. Mr Gregson, it seemed, was to be the head of this establishment so I soon got the necessary forms and put in an application.

This meant getting an up-to-date reference from the head at Broomfield and as it happened things began to happen quickly. He seemed concerned about this and the next day offered me a Grade I post to take responsibility for careers in the school. He made this quite tempting by saying that I would get an office and the assistance of a female member of staff to help out with the girls' side of the job. This, however, was not a job that I wanted and after some reflection put in for an interview for the post at Brentwood.

It was sometime in July that I went to Brentwood for the job interview and the appointment was for three pm, which was quite late in the day. It appeared that interviews for various posts had been going on all day and this post was probably at the bottom of the list.

There were four other applicants in the waiting room, two were relatively young men and went in first. They were obviously told that they needed more experience I think as they were not in the interview room very long and left afterwards. The third man seemed to be a staid sort of character and was in the interview room longer. He looked rather disgruntled when he came out.

In those days the senior handicraft advisor for Essex was a Mr I. Barber. Somehow he was not the most popular figure among the handicraft teachers because he had a rather forthright manner which seemed to offend some of them. As a new teacher I had found him very helpful and over the years I found no reason to fall out with him.

His job was to advise and he was in charge of a large area and had quite a bit of clout. I tended to take any advice and ideas from his department and treat them for what they were worth.

I wasn't aware that Mr. Barber would be part of the selection board but this was to be the case and wondered whether the disgruntled candidate had perhaps fallen foul of him at some time. When the fourth candidate was in the interview room for an extended time I began to get worried. When he came out he took his seat again and it became obvious that I had a serious rival for this job.

The board consisted of the headmaster Mr Gregson, four school governors and Mr Barber. The principal governor was a very elderly gentleman called Mr Hedley Walter and the comprehensive school would eventually be named after him.

I was of course asked quite a few pertinent questions of a general nature which went quite well I thought. When given the chance I stated that I also had a metalcraft certificate and that I hoped to get an appointment that would allow me to use this. I even envisaged a workshop setup, in which objects made by marrying wood and metal could be designed and made. The other point I made was that I hoped that in future craft subjects could be taken to examination level and I wanted to be part of such a setup. I wasn't sure whether or not I had over-enthused about this but they were honest statements and I had every intention of implementing my ideas if given the chance.

After some shuffling of notes and papers Mr Gregson asked me to wait outside while obvious deliberation took place.

Meanwhile I had a chat with the other teacher and it turned out that although he was a fully qualified craft teacher he had in recent years taught part-time physical training. He was hoping to revert to craftwork as he found P.T. was not so attractive as he was getting older.

As it turned out I was offered the post which I would be starting in September 1959. The headmaster took me over to the workshops and introduced me to the other craft teacher. He was a Mr Eric Makin. He was in fact and had been for many years the head of the woodwork department. He had other responsibilities as well, as he was in charge of a house.

In fact as I learned later he had been a pupil at the school and when he left school he went to a teacher's training college. Upon qualifying he had gone back to the school and had spent his whole working life there. He must have been in his late fifties at the time so this must have been quite a remarkable achievement of service.

There was to be one big downturn to my otherwise good day. The workshop, when I saw it, was a complete shambles, the benches were in terrible condition and many tools damaged, some beyond repair. Eric apologised for this, stating that the last occupant had been old and had retired the previous term. It seemed that odds and ends of people had been filling in since he had left. I could see that I would have my work cut out to get things in order for teaching in September. Towards the end of term I contacted Mr Barber at his office and told him of the situation and my need for practical help. He agreed to meet at the school and I told him that I was prepared to put two weeks of my summer holiday into getting the workshop improved. He agreed to supply replacements for the broken tools; these I had heaped onto one of the benches and a sorry lot they looked. I asked for suitable timber to replace the bench worktops and for some new woodwork units. He volunteered to supply a new woodwork lathe, as the existing one was clapped out and old fashioned. I cheekily asked if I could dispense with four of the woodwork benches and have in their place a metalwork bench. Surprisingly he agreed and as this would be a long bench fitted with eight metalwork vices, this to me was quite a coup. Perhaps the fact that I was willing to give up holiday time helped to persuade him in his generosity but at the end of the day I was very much helping myself as well.

Somewhere about this time, 1958 or so the divorce was finalised and Jo and I were married at Chelmsford at the Registry office. Her parents were there and a few friends but it really was a quiet affair.

The school at Brentwood did not become comprehensive straight away. At the time it was an amalgamation of two secondary modern schools, one boys' and next door a girls' version. The original buildings were quite old and it would be two to three years before the new part of the school was built. I had seen a copy of the plans and these included a practical block comprising a general metalwork room, another metalwork room with an engineering bias, a woodwork room and a drawing office for technical drawing classes. This all eventually came to pass but for two years or more I taught in the original workshop.

Eric Makin and I got on quite well and shared the practical workload fairly. I made him aware of that fact I hoped to do examination work and also had ambitions to do metalwork when the opportunity came.

When I asked the headmaster if I could have some extra money for materials to do some simple metalwork in my room, he was willing and keen. I was able to buy some sheet aluminium and strip metal, rivets and nuts and bolts and as I had the metalwork bench and vices we were able to do some combined wood and metalwork.

That first year beginning in 1958 I was given the first year A stream class. There were some bright boys among them and I was fortunate to continue with this group through their four years at the school. They would turn out to be my first examination group and when the time came I was able to enter them for their O-levels. We used the Oxford and Cambridge Examination Board as their syllabus suited our purposes. We entered thirteen candidates in that first exam year and twelve passed.

I remember that when the results came through, which was during the summer holidays that year, the head sent me a very complimentary letter which was a nice reward. Four of these boys stayed on at school to do A-levels in woodwork with success and then went on to teachers' training college and became craft teachers. Two did their training at Shoreditch College in London, and the other two went to Loughborough College in Leicestershire.

One of these was John Rolfe and I mention this because a few years later he would be teaching at the comprehensive school to which our younger sons went in Billericay, Essex.

In those early days at Brentwood I furthered my metalwork aspirations by running a club after school. These clubs were encouraged in those days and I felt it wise to do all I could to further my career.

As the summer of 1960 approached I also took over the junior cricket team. This turned out to be a real pleasure and I did it for two seasons. I took them for practices at first and realised that there was the nucleus of a good team there. One of these boys whose name was Brian Wiggett was particularly talented. They were all in the eleven, twelve year old age group and this boy was rather big for his eleven years. He was red headed and was surprisingly good with both bat and ball. During one practice I decided to bowl a few balls to him and hit him on the head, accidentally of course. He just shrugged it off and carried on. The team almost revolved round his ability and in the matches against other schools in the area we were seldom beaten.

On one occasion I did something rather silly by taking all eleven boys to an away match in my Morris van. Had we encountered a police presence during that trip I could have been in serious trouble and I often think how stupid that was.

Because of the nature of our work it was customary for craft teachers to have the first teaching period of the day for workshop maintenance. Our school days were strictly from 9am to 12pm, then an hour for lunch then from 1pm to 4pm from Monday to Friday. In those days this never varied and in earlier years buses, except service buses were not in evidence.

About 1961 a new scheme started as suitably qualified men were recruited as maintenance men on a full time basis. This meant that practical staff could and were to be used as form teachers. It was rather a shock to me when returning to school after the summer break to find myself in this position. The blow was softened to some extent as I was to have an assistant who in fact was a member of the domestic science staff. The class was my responsibility, however, and the new sparkling register had my name on it! A workshop was hardly the place for a form room as there was dust and grease about and not a suitable environment for young ladies. This problem was solved by using a domestic science room where there were tables and stools. We had no choice in the matter and things tended to get worse in later years, in fact for the last fifteen years of my teaching life I was coping with senior house forms on my own and using our drawing office as a form room.

This burdensome task was to some extent alleviated by the fact that I got to school early. Some of the form pupils who came by bus and also arrived early used to congregate near to the drawing office so I decided that they could come inside. There were several girls among these and they were very pleased to get inside and in fact used the opportunity to do their homework.

From Forty to Forty-Five

It was during 1961 and as I was approaching my fortieth birthday that we moved into the new practical block. I was granted a Grade II promotion and made head of the metalwork department. As I had been made aware of this for several weeks before it happened I had prepared schemes of work for the new venture. The workshop was a dream come true. I had managed to get two woodwork benches as part of the setup so it would be possible to unite the two subjects to some extent. The engineering workshop which adjoined had facilities for doing castings in aluminium, so this gave scope for some relatively simple pattern making. This of course also embraced woodwork and over the years I was able to do work with senior pupils that was very rewarding.

Improving the house in South Woodham was an ongoing venture and would be for many years to come.

During the years there Peter and David had integrated into the primary school very well. They both appeared to be quite bright and as Peter approached eleven thoughts of the eleven plus and eventual grammar school were being considered.

Quite out of the blue and I am not sure of the details he was offered a place at the Christ's Hospital School in Horsham.

I was informed of this by letter which stated that his mother was wanting this to happen as it was a very good opportunity which undoubtedly it was.

Christ's Hospital was well-known as the 'Blue Coat School' and was a public school with well-known credentials. They wore a distinctive uniform from a past age and were steeped in tradition as well as educational prowess.

It was never clear to me how this opportunity came about and I can only speculate as to its happening. I believe that one of Joyce's aunts was in a prominent position at the stately home of Lord Woolson, it could have been as housekeeper and her husband as butler or some such capacity.

It seemed that people in high positions in the land were allowed to present scholarships at intervals to Christ's Hospital. The school, I am sure, in its past had been heavily subsided by charitable institutions and important wealthy people who gave generously to its upkeep.

Well, for better or for worse Peter went to the school. It was too good an opportunity to miss I suppose but I can remember not being too happy about it. We didn't need charity as such as I expect if he had gone to the Chelmsford Grammar School he would have still attained his ambitions from there.

When David was nine he was also offered a place at the Christ's Hospital preparatory school and he went.

Both the boys, it must be said, did very well at Christ's Hospital and eventually went from there to university. Being a boarding school it was run to some extent on Spartan lines and wouldn't have suited everyone. Over those years I got the impression that Peter was less content with his lot than David but they both seemed reasonably happy when I visited them.

From South Woodham to the school in Horsham was quite a journey which entailed crossing London and measured about seventy miles. Visiting days were organised events and occurred twice a term. The problem was that having picked up the boys at the school I found that Peter had planned a run to some castle or other historical place which could mean considerably more mileage. It was always nice to see them of course and I am sure we all enjoyed these occasions. The complete day of course was quite tiring for me but very worthwhile. I was probably their most frequent visitor during those years as the grandparents had no means of transport and in any case were quite elderly.

When Simon was coming up to infant stage we produced two more sons. Timothy was born in February 1961 and Matthew in October 1962.

By this time my elder brother who had settled near Belfast had two children, a boy Eric and a girl Jean. He had in the meantime seriously embraced religion. This seemed alien to me as he had been anything but that way inclined during his youth and the run up to the war. He worked all his life over there as a heavy crane driver for the electricity board and they lived in council houses.

I went to visit them on several occasions over the years. He still had motorcycles including a trials bike. His main transport was a Reliant Robin which was a three-wheeler saloon car. They were rather small vehicles but very cheap to run and have been a popular mode of transportation for many people over the years.

My other brother Gordon had gone back to his roots after his war. He had had a tough time in the ongoing African campaign but at least he had survived. He lived and worked at Bassingbourn all his life and did related farm work. He worked early hours in all weathers to get seasonal foods to the London markets. In later life he had to have both hips replaced and this had been brought on by the heavy unpleasant work he did.

He and Freda also had two children, a boy Raymond and daughter Patricia. We visited them on occasions, they seemed to live a quiet life, and he was, I know, a good customer at the local pub.

Strangely enough sister Doreen and Dennis also had a boy and girl family. Michael was actually at Moulsham school when I did my first stint there. Rosalind, their daughter, happily married with children of her own still lives near Chelmsford and has kept in touch over the years.

Twin sister Vivien had joined the W.A.A.F quite early in the war. She married Ron who was a corporal cook in the R.A.F. and when she became pregnant had to leave the service. Ron came from farm working stock and was a Hampshire lad, and for several years after the war he was in charge of a large herd of pedigree cows. He lost this job when the farmer sold his land to make way for the M5 motorway which apparently bisected the land. He changed job then and worked for Sainsbury as a dispatch clerk at one of their depots near Basingstoke.

Ron was a nice easy-going character and a good family man. They were to end up with five daughters. So my twin had five daughters and I ended up with five sons which on reflection seems fine if a little odd.

The children had a good life at South Woodham, in those days it was a quiet restful place. They no doubt got into some mischief and I remember a meadow being set on fire so they must have been playing with matches on that occasion. There was a small but deep pond at the station end of the village and this was a source of worry to parents especially during the winter when it iced over. In spite of dire warnings Timothy has told me in recent years, they still played on and around this danger spot.

It was possible in those days to go for nice walks and sometimes have picnics. There was Hullbridge Road that led to the river Crouch and provided a delightful walk. There had in former years been a ferry there and you could see remnants of the staging points at both sides of the river which was very shallow at that point. There were some derelict boats about as well and a few others that people worked on. South Woodham today is a large satellite town, a busy place not at all like it was in the 1950s.

Teaching full time was quite hard work but in our new workshops with up-to-date facilities it was also very rewarding.

The school was still divided into four houses and they were named after the four districts of Brentwood. These were Thornden, Weald, Sawyer and Middleton and in the early days there was the usual competitive element among them. The Educational clever guys of the time were about to change this and sought a softly softly approach which more or less dictated that there should be no losers or winners. Our headmaster had certainly mellowed over the years and was not the person I had known back in Braintree. Sports days for instance became more like garden parties, some will say that this change-round was good and progressive but I must say I didn't agree.

Perhaps I was inclined to be a grumpy old person but having fought in a desperate war in which the whole nation had shown a great deal of fortitude, courage and backbone I could not see why a bit of competitive spirit was wrong.

During the 1960s and 1970s I had the responsibility of a senior house form. I would get the form each year as 4 Middleton 2 (4M2) as our house was Middleton and then keep them as 5M2 which was up to them becoming 6th formers if they stayed on. As stated before I used the adjacent drawing office as a form room. I had an arrangement each year that worked quite well. Getting to school early as I did, I was able to allow early pupils in as well and by and large they appreciated this! I was able to persuade a couple of girls, who for the most part were usually more helpful than the boys, to collect the form register and mark it for me in pencil as the pupils arrived. This helped me quite a lot as I was able to get my practical day organised in the workshop. I suppose it was an advantage, having fourteen to sixteen year olds as a form. The problem was that I never really got to know them as after registration they would disperse all over the school to their various academic classes. By or at fourteen, they had chosen their options which took them through the fourth and fifth and in many cases onto O- and A-level work. I used to get some of the boys from the form who happened to have chosen metalwork and this of course did happen.

It was about this time that I made a board game which became very popular with the boys in the form. It was a simple idea that consisted of an old drawing board which measured about 2ft long by 1ft 6ins wide which was marked out similarly to a football pitch. It was played with two coins of about 5/8" diameter which were the players and a smaller dice which was the ball. Around the edges of the board was screwed a thin strip of metal to stop the coins falling off. The players had a pusher made from wood or metal and the principles of the game related more to snooker than to football. I made up a set of strict rules and this game could develop into a very skilful one.

The boys formed team names after famous clubs and had a league and cup matches going. I was asked to play in these and as I had always been a Tottenham supporter played under that heading.

The goalposts were quite narrow and fitted into holes at each end. The game consisted of throw-ins, corners and penalties, one skill was to stymie your opponent (as in the original game of pool) which was all part and parcel of the game.

This game, of which my game was a version, originated in the North East of England. I read somewhere that miners and unemployed men of the time had played this and it definitely had roots there.

The boys themselves of course were able to make copies of this game and enjoyed doing so, they also fashioned their own pushers.

Over the years our boys have also played this game and now grandchildren do as well. I still have the original game including all the bits and pieces and I suppose it is a sort of family relic.

There is another relic that I have that goes back to my father. When he came home from the war in 1918 he brought back his service bayonet. I suppose this would have been illegal but in all the chaos and aftermath he managed to do it. In all the farm cottages and houses that we lived in it was always fixed to a wall or lodged on suitable nails. When my mother's home had to be sold up this came to me as I was the only family member who lived close. I offered to send it to Leslie in Ireland as he was the eldest son but being rather devout and reformed he refused the offer.

Today it comes under the category of a dangerous weapon and I probably should hand it in. On reflection, why should I? The stately homes of England and the gory castles of Scotland are full of weapons from the past. I remember on a visit to Scotland we went to Blair Atoll castle which has a stairway leading upwards and out of sight that is lined with axes, shields and swords of all descriptions which I thought was an impressive array. Quite recently I decided to get the blade engraved, the man in the shop was rather taken aback when I produced the weapon as I was carrying it up my sleeve with the hilt resting in the palm of my hand. The blade is made from cast steel and his machine was not able to cut into this but he was able to mark the blade reasonably well. This read SGT P.C. NIXON R.A.V.C. 1914-1918. I wish I knew more about him but for some unknown reason his parents and my mother never communicated after that war. They kept the post office at Nayland which is a town situated on the Essex-Suffolk border, for many years. They had two other sons who were both killed in the 1914-1918 conflict and their names are on the war memorial there. In the local church there is a wall plaque of the names of the local war dead and my father's as well as his brothers' names are there to be seen.

From Forty-Six to Fifty-One

The above period embraces the first years in our new environment at the Hedley Walter School. The man himself had died in the meantime and I gathered that he had been a school governor for many years when the boys' school was in operation. I got to know him fairly well as I was frequently to chauffeur him to various school functions. I remember on one occasion getting a note from him asking if I would be interested in dismantling an old chapel in Brentwood. He said this would be a good source of timber for the workshops as there were oak partitions and pews which would be worthwhile rescuing. The headmaster allowed me to take several senior boys and we ended up with some useful well-seasoned timber.

Eric Makin had also by this time retired as he had reached the age of sixty five. His wife was Welsh and they had planned their retirement. They spent a lot of their time when holidaying in North Wales, where his wife's parents lived.

During the school years that I knew him he was very rarely absent for any reason and I thought really deserved a well-earned rest. Unfortunately he died of natural causes within a year which seemed such a shame.

An experienced woodwork teacher had taken his place and another younger woodwork man had also been appointed and was installed in my previous workshop in the old school.

I was by now teaching metalwork full time in the general purpose craft room. The other metalcraft room which adjoined was equipped with engineering machinery. It had a large turret lathe similar to an industrial one, also it had a milling machine and casting facilities, the latter was mainly a furnace for melting aluminium.

128

A new appointment was made and he was an engineering graduate from Loughborough University. He was in his mid-thirties so I presumed he had taken his qualifications late in life. His name was Gledhill and we got on quite well together. He made little use of the engineering facilities, however, and he taught metalwork to classes in the same way that I did. I always thought this a little wasteful and I found myself using the facilities in his room, especially the casting, more then he did. We worked in tandem for many years and things went well enough. We shared the examination work but I did the bulk of the O- and A-level work. He seemed happy to concentrate on the new trendy C.S.E. exams and together we were required to set internal papers for a Mode 1 version of the new C.S.E. exams. For myself I have never been in favour of the C.S.E. system especially as it was in those days. For teachers to be able to set their own examination papers and to be able to tailor the questions to the pupils' needs seems wrong. We as teachers of course did as we were told by our superiors and had to follow the trend. A pupil who obtained a grade 1 pass in any subject was said to have a qualification equal to a G.C.E. O-level. This in my opinion was not a true reflection and I feel that many employers of the day were duped with new employees not being able to cope as expected. The old adage that you cannot make a silk purse from a pig's ear comes to mind and could not be truer.

Well it stands to reason that everyone cannot be or would expect to be a University student. People who are more suited to a more menial type of life are happier doing that. Someone has to do those jobs so what is wrong with fitting the right shaped pegs into suitable holes?

Of course the minimum wage for all should be much more adequate as all are entitled to a decent standard of living. Pensions for the old should also be at a high enough rate so the recipients should not require to go for handouts, to live reasonably comfortably. This to my mind is not asking too much but I suppose that would be to live in an ideal world which is far from being the case.

When Eric Makin retired our house (Middleton) was taken over by Fred Griffith (no 's' on the end if you please) and he was the overall head of art in the new setup and specialised in pottery. Over the next fifteen years and into eventual retirement we were to become close workmates as well as good friends. We had a lot in common, as we liked all forms of sport and had a similar competitive nature. We became Bridge partners and were quite a formidable pairing. We often played Scrabble during lunchtimes at school. We found ourselves pitting our wits against the head of English and also the head librarian, often with success and these forays were very highly contentious. As a senior member of the house he relied a lot on my co-operation and we were a good team. On Tuesdays of each week our house was responsible for the running of the school and the practical staff all teamed together to do the duties. This included the domestic science and needlework teachers as well as the art and craft teachers.

In a modern comprehensive setup of over eleven hundred pupils these duties had to be well organised and they were. They started before 9 o'clock and included playtime and lunchtime supervision as well as a four o'clock bus duty.

So each of the four houses had a duty day, this meant that Friday was the prerogative of all the staff who were not attached to a house. The headmaster was supposedly in charge on Fridays backed by the various deputy heads, sports personnel and ancillary staff. This in fact turned out to be a disorganised rabble, not too strong a word, and the pupils seemed to know and take advantage of this. You might say for example that many more cigarettes were smoked in the toilets on Fridays than any other days.

Having some influence in house matters I was able to avoid lunchtime duties. Many preferred this duty as a free lunch went with it. I preferred to take a packed lunch and always did. I was thus able to prepare afternoon lessons and quite often pupils came in to do casting work as the sand moulding facilities were limited. Some senior boys who needed to do extra coursework would also avail themselves of this opportunity. My form pupils would quite often come in to play their football board game as well. For many years I found myself doing one of the less pleasant duties which was supervising pupils on to their respective buses immediately after school. The children had to be lined up at their stations for this and ushered aboard their buses. I always thought this to be a daft idea and could never understand why the pupils could not have been allowed to just walk on to the vehicles as they arrived. It seemed the powers that be thought otherwise and the bus companies represented by the drivers preferred the more military approach. There was always the inevitable pushing from behind which made the duty difficult at times. When dealing with large numbers as we were why make life more complicated? The children were all between 11 and 16 years and could I am sure have been prevailed upon to act as young adults in a civilised way and board the buses in an ordinary manner.

My other duty on Tuesdays was the fifteen minute playground one. Two or three of us were on patrol and I included the boys' toilet block on my beat. I suppose that being a non-smoker I did my best to suppress this awful habit. I worried about the influence that smoking had on younger pupils, but there was never a chance that you could stop it altogether even though in those days pupils caught smoking could be severely punished.

With hard work the old house at South Woodham was becoming quite respectable both inside and out. I had got to the stage where I had built on a sun room area at the rear and a lean-to garage on the side which was big enough to house my workbench as well as the car. This of course was gradually increasing the value of the property. I tended to use any spare cash for materials, so we were in a position to develop the property without having to borrow any money.

When Simon was about five we decided to send him to a private school at Danbury called Heathcote. Peter and David were at school in Sussex and were being paid for so it seemed fair to do our best for Simon. He went to Heathcote for several years but in all honesty didn't seem to benefit much from being there. From five years until he eventually left secondary school at fourteen he never shone at school and his reports, which were mainly dire, confirmed this. He tended to have an introspective attitude which we found difficult to understand, because he seemed happy enough in himself and as proved in his later life he actually knew what his capabilities were and what he wanted to do with his life.

When Tim and Matt were infants Jo joined a young mothers' club that met quite frequently in the village hall. All the infants seemed to be monitored and I think the club was supervised like a clinic. It seemed to work quite well and Jo became quite friendly with other mothers and I recollect that there were baby shows and other activities going on. She became particularly friendly with Elsie Rogers, who had a son Paul and we have remained family friends even to this day. The boys grew up together and I often took Tim, Matt and Paul to the park at Maldon which was about ten miles away. As they grew they supported their favourite football teams. Paul's relatives had connections with West Ham FC, Tim followed me as a Tottenham supporter and Matt favoured Chelsea. I remember them playing football at Maldon dressed in their respective team outfits.

The medical surgery in those early days was held in a room in a private house. The actual doctors' practice was at Wickford and at the time the doctors were an elderly Dr Frew and his two sons. They came to the village on set days and at set times and the older doctor came most frequently. He seemed to be very good and a kindly person and the scheme worked well. Eventually a proper medical unit was built in the village as gradual expansion was taking place.

When this happened Jo (the two boys by this time being at school) was employed as a secretary-cum-nurse at the clinic and this went on for several years. She seemed happy to be doing something practical as well as useful and appreciated a chance to keep her hand in at her chosen profession.

These early years at South Woodham were idyllic in some ways and it was hardly necessary to go out of the village for supplies. There was a well-stocked grocery and a delivery service. The greengrocers was within walking distance and his wares were varied and always fresh. Near the station was the local hostelry and I think it was called the Railway Arms. We had little to do with this establishment as our money had to be prudently spent.

Near the railway crossing was a paper and confectionery shop that seemed to do a good trade in the early mornings. It was run very well by an elderly lady who eventually died. The people who took over were not nearly as successful with the business and it declined quite rapidly which seemed a shame at the time.

As I said, we had become friends with Elsie and Don Rogers, who actually lived on the far side of the level crossing in quite a pleasant bungalow. Don for many years had worked for British Rail and was a joiner, I think a lot of his work was to do with refurbishment and service at stations and they had the luxury of free rail travel. They had an elder son, Michael, who was in his middle teens. He was a very hard worker and earned weekend money working for a coalman, which entailed delivering coal from a railway siding onto a lorry and distributing it around the district. It drove poor Elsie to distraction when he would come home black and filthy but he was happy and the money was good.

In the centre of the village was a large house with quite extensive grounds. The owner was a businessman stationed in London and the family appeared to be quite wealthy. They spent a lot of time in the village and they grew a lot of produce in the large garden. Simon somehow managed to get weekend work there and in time took over the running of the chicken side of the smallholding. I remember he often came home with eggs that had no shells and this was part of the perks.

The large house mentioned above was the first to be sold to developers that would eventually turn the friendly village of South Woodham into a satellite town. This took several years to come about and many local property owners were to benefit considerably when they sold out.

From Fifty-Two to Fifty-Seven

Another member of staff with whom I became quite friendly was Lees Howorth who was head of the school music department. He had been at the school for many years and was a very affable type of man and a bachelor who lived in quite a large house in Brentwood with his elderly mother. In spite of having a speech impediment he was always well respected by the pupils. I suppose he had probably taught the parents of many of them and was almost an institutional figure.

I had contacts with the theatres and concert halls in London and was able to get blocks of seats at considerably reduced prices. This was a good opportunity for staff that were interested and I can remember pleasant evenings at the Festival Hall and even sometimes at Covent Garden.

His department of course put on school concerts and entertainments which were always well-attended. At one time I got two or three senior boys to make a set of tubular bells from brass tubes. I did some research on tube size and methods of obtaining suitable lengths. The length was critical for tuning and I remember Lee tapping the suspended tubes until they sounded right. It was a good project and a useful addition to the school orchestra. There was one thing during these times that became the bane of my life. The music stands were metal and not too sturdy and we seemed to get a steady stream of these damn things in for repair.

It was at about this time the headmaster Mr Gregson was badly hurt in a car accident. His legs and back were quite severely damaged and he was never really fit again. The full details of the accident were never known. He did not drive himself and he was being taken to a conference by another member of staff when it happened. He returned as Head for quite some time and managed to do quite a lot of his work from home.

This meant quite a lot of toing and froing by his secretary between the school office and his home which was quite close to the school. One day I received a note from the headmaster asking if I could spare a half hour or so after school as he had something to discuss with me as a departmental head.

He had, it appeared, received a directive from Essex Education Authority saying that woodwork and metalwork would eventually be phased out. This was mainly due to rising costs of wood and metal and as numbers in the schools were increasing these costs could not be maintained. In the directive it suggested that craft teachers should consider plastics and fibreglass as alternatives and also lean towards science and technology as alternatives to traditional craft teaching. I was not altogether surprised to hear this as there had been mumblings about change in craft circles for some time. He went on to say that we as craft teachers should be educating the children for leisure pursuits rather than work-allied ones as it was predicted that many young people would not be able to find full-time work in the future.

My inner reaction to all this was to assume that these changes would not happen in my time as I was hoping to retire after teaching for thirty years and I had completed twenty-six.

He gave me details of a course on fibreglass canoe making which was taking place at a local college in the Romford area on several consecutive Saturday mornings. He hoped that Brian Gledhill and myself would attend this course as a gesture to our attitude towards change. In fact Brian and I did enrol for this course and we found it interesting enough and between us we made quite a passable canoe. We both agreed that the materials and chemicals involved were unsuitable for young people to use and a suitable well-ventilated work area would be essential for the work. Handling the fibreglass and fixing the layered construction with the liquid glue required a good degree of skill and one needed special gloves and face-masks to do the work. The chemicals used were quite toxic and fibreglass sheets were hazardous to inhale.

When we reported back to Mr Gregson after the course we pointed out these facts. We also said that the materials for doing the work were costly and by the time preventative clothing was bought there would be little expense saved.

He was not very happy with our findings but as Brian and I had put forward a valid argument there was little he could do about it.

While he was chair bound he had quite a lot of time to watch educational programmes on the television and soon after the above semi-fiasco he came up with another idea which he put into place without any consultation with his craft staff at all. He appointed a youngish teacher who it appeared was very good at sculptural work. He showed some photographs of this man's work which showed very beautiful and impressive work. The theory was that small blocks of wood such as lime, mahogany and other suitable timbers could be had at reasonable prices and this seemed a good thing. I pointed out that this approach to woodwork would not be good without stringent emphasis on safety and hoped this new teacher realised this. The headmaster merely said that the man was experienced and also that much of the work could be done with wood rasps and appropriately shaped files. At this I gave up and in the coming term this man started work.

He was ensconced in my previous workshop which was away from the main craft block in the old part of the school which meant that he was isolated to some extent. After a couple of weeks the maintenance man came to me saying that he was having problems with damaged gauges and other carving tools and was having to spend so much time in this one workshop that his other commitments were being neglected. Then the thing that I feared most happened. The head's main secretary was a very efficient matronly type of lady and had taken upon herself to do the odd first aid requirements. This was usually administering the odd aspirin and band aids on scraped knees and she coped quite well. At about this time I received an urgent message to go to the office where this lady was busy mending up a nasty gash in a child's thumb. She was really angry, saying that she recently had five such wounds to deal with from this junior workshop and as head of craft I had to do something about it. It appeared that three of the cuts had required stitches at the local hospital and she stated that she could not cope with this serious situation. After calming her down somewhat I agreed to go over to the workshop and have a talk with the new teacher. I also made it clear that she was to report all five incidents to our headmaster which she agreed to do.

After this things improved for a few weeks. The headmaster's solution was to ask the head handicraft advisor for help. During this same term on Friday mornings we had senior boys in the workshops and the new teacher had 4B to cope with. As stated before all the classes in the school were mixed ability forms as by this time streaming at the Hedley Walter Comprehensive School had long gone.

Not very far from our school in the village of Hutton was a semi-Borstal type of school which took boys and girls from broken homes. Many of them seemed to be sad cases of neglect but there was also a core of hardened tough youngsters. All the local comprehensive schools had to take a percentage of these people who were all in the fourteen- to sixteen-year-old range. Of course the local technical and grammar schools were exempt from this and our type of school which already had the lower end of pupil ability had as usual the rough end of the stick.

So our mixed ability senior classes had to absorb these pupils and there were some of course who were a bad influence on weaker members of these groups.

One Friday matters came to a head in the junior workshop where this senior age group form were being instructed by the new sculpture teacher.

I suppose it is true to say that all children tend to be impatient and in my experience I tended to have schemes of work that produced some early progress. If for instance a child starts to work on a small cube of wood that looks reasonably attractive and a couple of hours of chiselling and filing it looks worse than it had been to begin with, this would be disheartening to say the least. With sharp tools it could be easy to remove too much wood with disastrous results and the whole concept (if there had been one to begin with) would readily disintegrate.

To be a very successful sculptor in any material I think one has to have a gift and feeling that not many people have. This man had undoubtedly that quality as could be seen by the work he was capable of doing. To get balanced and aesthetic shapes and to obtain the beautiful smoothness and finish required from young adults was another matter and I don't think this was possible to attain.

The next Friday when we all had the same senior groups in the workshops there was serious indiscipline in the other workshop. It seemed that the three or four unruly types from the home school were throwing pieces of wood or probably their work pieces at each other and a minor riot was ensuing. The maintenance man came over to get me to help sort this out. He stayed with my class while I went. It was getting near the end of the morning session so when I arrived at the workshop I suggested that the teacher pack up for the morning and that he and I would have a problem sorting chat when the class had gone. The whole problem resolved itself that day as the teacher had had enough and he decided to leave.

A few months later he wrote to me from Cornwall saying that he had started a craft studies and workshop business that was beginning to flourish so all had ended well.

It was soon after this episode that Mr Gregson gave up the headship and was replaced by Miss Jones. She was at the school for about six months and eventually left under a cloud of scandal that was well-publicised at the time in the press. She seemed a very pleasant person to me and I could not understand how such an intelligent woman could get her life into such a tangled mess.

She was at the school when Lee Howarth and the music department put on a version of the musical 'Joph'. His deputy who was an energetic youngish lady was determined to involve as many people as possible and most of the staff were raked into singing in the chorus.

This included myself and many others who I am sure were not gifted vocally but the enthusiasm engendered was such that we decided to have a go. Miss Jones was no exception and at the time seemed a model headmistress.

138

Our dress was very simple as it consisted of a folded white sheet with a hole cut out for one's head and arms. The rest was folded rather like an oval burnoose and tied around the midriff. The whole production was a huge success really and played to parent audiences for several evenings.

Sometime at about this time, the early seventies, Jo's father retired from his job as a railway employee. They almost immediately sold the house at Chadwell Heath and bought a bungalow in South Woodham. It was about a quarter of a mile from us in Hullbridge Road and was quite a nice place with a large garden. Jo's father was quite tall and heavily built; she had not got on well with him as a child as he was quite a forceful character. Overall, her childhood was not a happy one and I understand she was frequently sent to stay with her grandparents at Kelvedon which is about ten miles from Chelmsford. He was quite an intelligent man and was fond of good music and I found him easy enough to get on with. No doubt he had mellowed somewhat in old age, and he seemed quite content, he was very good at gardening and this kept him busy.

He was not, however, destined to have a long retirement and after they had been there about two years he had some sort of seizure and died in bed.

During the twelve years or so in which I travelled from South Woodham to the school at Brentwood I must have clocked up many thousands of miles as the daily journey was thirty-six miles. I remember selling the Morris van in the early Sixties and it had done ninety thousand miles and had served me well. From then to retirement in 1979 I purchased a run of Renault cars which were all new. I chose that make because there was a Renault dealership at Wickford which was convenient and they always gave me a good trade-in price.

For four years during this time I was also taking adult classes in woodwork which was quite a pleasant experience and a change from my metalwork routine. The class consisted mainly of middle-aged men and some women who were keen to make items of furniture for their homes. The provided their own materials but I was responsible for the tool maintenance and tuition. These classes and many others came under the auspices of the Evening Institute and had to be held in the old part of the school. This meant that I was once again teaching in my original woodwork room. These classes were quite well paid and I tended to keep the money for car renewal and running expenses.

The headmistress at the village school at South Woodham was there for many years during our stay and at various times taught all our boys. She was very popular and did a very good job all round. I can remember her name which was Mrs Hicks, and she was a motherly type of lady. She retired while we still lived in the village and a headmaster took her place.

The village school was sited on the Hullbridge Road and was only a few minutes' walk from our house, Avenue Villa. The new headmaster in fact had a house built on a plot of land that was opposite our house. I think the property, on reflection, was more of a ranch type bungalow and was quite grand. We got the impression that this was a private venture and not a related school property.

As his bungalow progressed I got to know the new headmaster quite well. Seeing the place grow was quite an experience and we often chatted about building generally and particularly of the new innovations that he was having built in. I think his name was Mr. Lowe and he also had the job of dealing with an expanding child population as the village was about to grow rapidly.

In fact plans had already been passed to the building conglomeration known as 'Coopers Estates' to build several hundred houses in and around South Woodham. This of course had its minuses and plusses for the locals and in any case was to be a steamroller operation that would create a new town.

We were to benefit immediately as our access track that had been for years used by tractors and other farm vehicles was to be a new road leading to this 'Coopers Development'. Within days we had a new concrete road with a sewer connection, pavements both sides with a lowered access to the garageway and it just seemed like a miracle.

I think that Mr Lowe must have been aware of this when he bought the land for his property as of course he also benefited from this development.

This improved the value of our property very considerably and meant that I could install a proper bathroom and toilet facilities, which in fact I made a priority.

Son Simon, who had spent the latter years at Sandon School near Chelmsford was coming to the end of his secondary school education. The leaving age was fourteen at that time and his reports were not at all encouraging so we were not sure about his future.

However, quite unknown to us he had made some serious decisions of his own! We were taken completely by surprise when on a Saturday morning at about this time we heard a heavy knock at the door. At the door was a large soldier with many stripes and badges who declared himself to be recruiting Sergeant Fowler and could he have a few words with us.

He declared that Simon had been enquiring about a career in the army medical corps and had been such a nuisance with his persistence that they had decided to take it seriously. At fourteen, of course, he would become a boy soldier and had to have the full backing of parents and therefore the sergeant had to be aware of the full facts. On this Saturday morning Simon was working in the village so we were rather in a dilemma. On reflection, although feeling a bit stupid with this development, we could see no reason why he should not follow his own wishes as regards to his future. We therefore listened to the pros and cons about junior army life. It seemed that there was a clause which allowed an unhappy recruit to leave after six months which seemed a sensible idea.

To his credit Simon made the army his career for many years and eventually reached the rank of Major. He married Diane and they had four children, two girls and two boys. He started serious study later on in his life and procured good qualifications and now lectures on the subjects that he also did in the army. This was teaching students on the mechanical side of surgery I think and certainly he has had a very satisfying career.

When father-in-law died in the mid-seventies, this heralded an enforced change of direction for us as a family.

As a married couple they had had a rather turbulent life as he had a forceful character and had over the years had an adverse effect on Jo his daughter as well as on his wife. All this had left Jo's mother in a neurotic state of health and when he died she for some obscure reason refused to live in their bungalow on her own. She in fact moved in with a friend who lived nearby and was a widow.

At this time a local builder was completing a new house adjacent to our house on a vacant plot. It was quite a large house very well built with a mansard roof and designed to have an integral garage. Jo and I came to the conclusion that if we could sell our house and the vacant mother-in-law's bungalow we could buy this new house with the combined sums.

The builder and I agreed a price of £8,500 for this new property. He explained that it would take about ten weeks to complete which gave us time to get the two properties on the market. He agreed to turn the integral garage into an extra room so that mother-in-law would have her separate living room with an adjacent bathroom and toilet.

Since we now had ownership of Avenue Villa and the plot next door I was able to move legally the boundary fence between the two properties. I simply took a copy of the new property plans to our solicitors in Wickford and told them that I was reducing the Avenue Villa plot by twenty-five feet which would be added to the new property which we had decided to call 'Mansard'. This turned out to be a simple matter of registry and was soon done. The advantage to us was that the extra land could be used for the erection of an external garage which I put in place a few months after we eventually moved in.

The bungalow sold quite quickly as it was a nice property with a well-cultivated and stocked garden, courtesy of father-in-law's talent and efforts.

Selling Avenue Villa was not quite so easy. We needed to get £4000 for it to break comfortably even and this was proving difficult.

We had got to know quite well a young married couple, they had a boat that they worked on at weekends near the ferry at the end of Hullbridge Road. He was a keen motorcyclist so we had that in common; he had a fairly mundane job but his wife on the other hand had quite a well-paid professional post in London. It seemed they lived in rented accommodation locally and she travelled up to the city every day by train.

They got to know that we were trying to sell Avenue Villa and showed some interest in buying it. It seemed that their combined assets were about £2000, so quite out of character I decided to offer them a deal. I proposed that I would accept their £2000 as a deposit, that I would raise the price to £4,500 and that they could pay the balance by monthly payments of £200 until the amount was paid off. This of course would have to be legally tied up with our solicitors.

After a few days deliberation they agreed to this and so gradually the process came together to everyone's satisfaction. It of course took two years for them to complete the payments and to their credit we had no difficulties at all with this, he would turn up regularly at the end of each month with the £200. I suppose they did quite well out of the transaction and it meant that our arrangements could also flourish, which they did. To them it was, I suppose, like a first-time buy and a step on the property ladder.

When the new road was completed it became Pertwee Drive and of course it was a boon to us, particularly the access to a main sewer. To build manholes and lay the four inch pipe work was a new building experience for me. I had, however, had the experience of helping Stan Hart do the drainwork at the bungalow at Wallace Crescent in Chelmsford. My main job there was to do the manual work and we were in a hurry in those days. The drain work at Avenue Villa was fairly straightforward and I managed to build the three manholes and arrange the pipes.

My mother and stepfather still lived in nearby Danbury, she by this time was in her mid-seventies. Stepfather was about ten years her junior and when I told him about the drainwork he volunteered to dig the trenches for me that connected the manholes. This was a great help and speeded up the work considerably. As he dug the trenches I was able to work out the correct fall or shape and could get the concrete bed in place on which the drainpipes would be laid.

So all went very well but I must say that I was rather apprehensive about the official inspection. The inspector from the County Building Department had agreed to do the testing early before I went to work. On the day it was pouring buckets of rain and the earth in parts had fallen back into the trenches so that he was unable to inspect the joints properly. He was able to see inside the manhole nearest the house and I remember him standing there with a tennis ball in his hand. The main test was to roll a ball along the pipes to make sure there was no clogging and this also tested the slope from the first manhole to the furthest which was at the end next to the mains sewer connection. I remember at this point he said, "I presume you have done this work yourself for yourself so I guess it has to be good". With that he put the ball back in his pocket, said goodbye and scooted off back quickly to his car to get out of the rain. So that was that.

The next project was to turn our third bedroom into a bathroom. I actually found this to be a pleasure rather than a chore; being a metalworker the pipework in copper was very easy to do. The various elbow joints and other connections were all pre-soldered in the form of Yorkshire fittings so that with due care and the use of a blow lamp the work was relatively simple.

The third bedroom was the same size as our kitchen and immediately above it. This made the drainage problems fairly simple as the first manhole was in close proximity. The new toilet was in fact on the ground floor, situated where the old chemical toilet had been, which meant that this pipework was also easy to do and it was easy to connect this to the same manhole.

We bought the bathroom suite from a specialist shop in Wickford and were also able to buy a large 'Sadia' electric heater. This was fitted with two elements, one for normal household use and a larger section for heating bath water so it suited our requirements very well.

What a pleasure it was to have these new facilities and we enjoyed these simple amenities very much after the many years of making do with primitive ones.

When we eventually moved into the large new house next door it was also quite an experience. It was fitted out very well with all mod cons which included the luxury of central heating. Of course the cost of running this house rose considerably but we managed quite well. In those days the house taxation and the water bill were lumped together and in the early days in Avenue Villa these costs were minimal as we were on an unmade road.

Mother-in-law settled in with us very well and of course the fact that we had this large new property without any sort of mortgage was due in no small part to the selling of her bungalow.

Simon settled very well into his army life and we were invited to Aldershot to his passing-out parade which was quite a busy day as it meant a long drive. He was quite happy to progress into the mainstream army and trained to be a surgical technician and he remained in that department of the Medical Corps for most of his army service.

Peter had by this time left Christ's Hospital and had been to Exeter University and then on to teaching. He seemed very content with his chosen career and he taught in independent schools after a short spell in a state middle school. He was very successful at writing and producing dramatic works and we were invited to some of his productions over the years.

For quite a few years he seemed content to live in at these schools and be a bachelor. It was while teaching at a prep school near St. Albans in Hertfordshire that he met Lyn who was to become his wife. She had two young sons, one of whom was a prominent actor in a play that he was putting on and their lives, that is Peter and Lyn's, progressed together from there and they have had a very happily married life from then on. The sons who of course are now grown up with families of their own have had very varied and successful lives.

When David left Christ's Hospital he went to Clare College in Cambridge to read Mathematics. He stayed on an extra year to do his Diploma in Education and he did teach for a short time at a grammar school in Saffron Walden. He found teaching junior pupils mathematics rather tedious, especially all the marking, and so he left. He did research work at Marconi in Chelmsford for a few years but when he was transferred to working on underwater weaponry he left. David was inclined to be fairly religious and I suppose this job pricked his conscience.

We lived in the new house for only two years. The journey for me to Brentwood was becoming rather tedious and I had had it in mind to move nearer the school for my last few years of teaching for some time. By now both the younger boys were due to go to secondary school so a move would not affect their education unduly.

There was a man in South Woodham who ran an electronics firm and on several occasions he had shown an interest in our house. It was a very nice property and somewhat different to the mass-produced houses that Coopers Estates were mushrooming around! So I had no difficulty in agreeing a price with him. There was some haggling and he cheekily suggested I should pay the interest on a building loan that he would require. In the end we settled for a price of £12,500 and we were in a position to find a suitable place in our chosen venue of Billericay. This small town was about four miles from Brentwood and had a comprehensive school for Timothy and Matthew to attend. So, it was a question of finding a four-bedroom house that suited our requirements and as our sale was agreed this was not too difficult a problem.

We found a nice house, via an estate agent, that was situated in a cul-de-sac and in a quiet area of Billericay. It was set up high above the road with a type of rock garden at the front which, like the garageway, sloped steeply upwards.

The place was really ideal in most respects and I believe we paid £11,000 for it. The only snag was the central heating system which worked by a hot air ducted process. The makers were a Scandinavian firm called Husquarra and although the principles were good the actual gas heater could be very temperamental. This proved to be a hindrance as Jo's mum spent a lot of her time in her room which really did need heating. In the end we bought her a three-switch electric fire that she could use if the heating failed which it often did.

Our eventual move from South Woodham would have been in 1973 and Tim and Matt started their senior school education that September. The journey for me was much easier and in most respects everything was for the better. Jo decided to do some nursing at the local burns unit that was attached to the hospital. She elected to do two nights and was in charge of the ward and that was quite a responsible job.

Jo's mum or Gran was not too happy with the move and I guess that having three age groups or generations under one roof was not ideal. She was by now in her late seventies but quite fit and agile for her age. It was at this time that she had appendicitis and withstood the operation very well. During that winter she became rather difficult to cope with, as she often wanted to go out when the paths were icy. The slope from our frontage was very treacherous for a start and the last thing we wanted was a broken bone or more.

From Fifty-Five to Sixty

This period of time encompasses my last four years of teaching and the first year of retirement. My friend Fred Griffith was rather a social climber and had met two accountants who had high-powered jobs at Fords of Dagenham. They both lived in executive-style houses in Danbury and it appeared they were quite keen bridge players. So we started to play for one evening a week at our respective homes; these were very pleasant occasions and went on for about four years. The competition was quite fierce at times but Fred and I usually won mainly because one of the opposition was inclined to gamble and bridge is just not a gambling game.

By this time our headmaster was a Mr Fry and he had assumed the reins very competently after the Miss Jones fiasco. He tended to allow the departments to function on their own and seemed to appreciate his good fortune in having a sound staff.

He did emphasise the fact that craftwork as such would be phased out over the coming years and sooner rather than later. This did not worry me too much as I had always hoped to retire after thirty years and that would be 1979 having qualified in 1949. At that time we were still doing examination work at O- and A-levels with the associated examination board as well as mode 3 C.S.E. It was a sad thing to happen as the majority of pupils really enjoyed their craftwork and it gave them a break from their more enforced academic work.

During these latter years I had classes of third year girls (14-year-olds) doing jewellery. The craft block was timetabled to take the whole of the third year for a two period session on Friday afternoons. All the art and craft rooms were involved and the boys did cookery or fabric work. The sessions were half-termly which meant about

148

a six week period which was not very long. I decided that I would get the girls to design a simple brooch or a pendant. It was possible to buy silver chains and pin-type fasteners to solder onto brooches and this worked quite well for these short term sessions. A few of the girls were difficult as they were at an awkward period of their education and were in the process of choosing options to take them onto their final years including the sixth form.

I had a serious bust up with one little or rather large madam whose design for a brooch was in the form of a swastika. I objected to this on principle but she insisted on this idea and refused to do anything else and got quite nasty. At the end of that first lesson, one of the other girls said that this girl was a member of a Hell's Angels group who met with their noisy motorcycles at weekends. The girl herself was quite big and well-developed for her age and I suppose would have looked much older in suitable clothing than she was. It seemed that the swastika brooch was to be a present for one of the male members of the group.

I got on well with the lady who was deputy head and in charge of the girls and female staff in the school and told her of this problem. She was quite sympathetic and simply transferred the offending girl to another group and I had a more amenable replacement.

In the past I had had several senior girls who had chosen craftwork as an option. They were usually artistic pupils and were interested in jewellery design and over the years produced some good work. I had been able to obtain a small kiln and suitable materials so that we could do enamelling on sheet copper. There was a small acid vat in my workshop which was essential for cleaning copper. The boys doing exams had to have a working knowledge of metals and their properties. C.S.E. pupils often made copper articles for their coursework so the diluted acid in the vat was an essential part of the workshop equipment.

To enamel on copper was not an easy process. To be successful the metal involved had to be completely chemically clean, even a fingerprint would cause a failure on the fusion of the enamel powder to the copper. This meant that we had a fair percentage of failures with disappointing consequences.

During his four years at the Billericay Comprehensive Tim seemed to work quite well, at least I don't remember him being in trouble.

Matthew on the other hand was a disaster and always seemed to be in bother with the teachers. He was inclined to be clownish rather than nasty and always ready to be involved with stupid ideas, not always of his own making. Being like a sister school I knew quite a few of the staff that taught him and his prankish behaviour was quite an embarrassment at times. He had one redeeming feature and showed an interest in baking and cooking. Towards the end of his schooling he spent most of his time helping out in the school kitchens. They thought he was great and clubbed together to buy him a small present when he left.

Whereas Tim declined any further education, Matt had an interview to attend a bakery course at a college near Romford. He stayed the course and eventually got a diploma in bakery which in fact led to a job as a commis chef at the Royal Garden Hotel in London. I think he found this job and the shift work it entailed not very satisfying and a rather lonely experience.

Tim, after he left school, was not at all interested in a formal career of any sort. He eventually left home for a hippy existence that went on for several years. He was in a squat with similar-minded friends in Bristol and also spent time in Wales under similar circumstances. He was very influenced by the pop music of the times and all that that meant. It seemed that there were handouts and methods of procuring easy money in those days which seemed all wrong and encouraged a loose type of life for many young people.

This in a way led to Matthew leaving his job in London as he was I am sure influenced by Tim and his easy way of life.

So for many years we had two wandering hippy sons. I think Jo probably felt this more than I did. We felt that they should have made more of their early lives. They certainly had quite a caring, normal childhood and I still feel resentful about their behaviour at this time.

They both have a much steadier lifestyle in their middle years so things have improved in that respect.

150

So at the age of fifty-nine I left teaching. We stayed in Billericay for several months but it was always our intention to retire to a quiet country area. Jo and I spent several weekends looking around in Suffolk either at new developments or more established bungalows. The American Air Force had several large stations in Suffolk, there was one at Bentwaters, the place in which we had lived in the late Nineteen Twenties. This was a massive place at the time and very busy and noisy with the sound of many aircraft. I think we became disillusioned for a time and put off our house hunting for the 1979-1980 winter period. In the Spring we set off to explore Norfolk with determination and gusto and visited quite a few properties over a short period of time. It came down to a choice in the end between a new bungalow in Burnham Market and a more natural place on the outskirts of Fakenham. The one at Burnham Market was more up to date of course but part of a complex of bungalows that were overlooked by taller houses at the back. The Fakenham property was rather larger with a nice garden on three sides and open fields at the back. I suppose I was also swayed by the fact that there was golf course nearby as I had been considering taking up the game. Well, we both happily settled for this place in the end and as there was a thriving W.I. in the town Jo was quite happy with that.

Towards the end of our stay in Billericay Mother-in-law decided to move out, she was by now in her late seventies. Tim and Matt were into loud pop music as most teenagers of the time were and I suppose that three generations in one house was not an ideal scenario. She moved into a small self-contained bungalow not too far away and she seemed much happier for this move. There were a few contemporaries in the same complex which meant she could make more friends and she seemed much more content. At the age of eighty-two she died after a short illness which was sad as she had a traumatic life with a husband who seemed to be neurotic to say the least.

Until I was sixty-five we had to manage financially on my teachers' pension. So we had to be somewhat frugal during those first years but once we had the supplement of our state pensions we were quite well off. The house in Billericay sold well partly I think because it was within walking distance of the railway station and a direct route that way to London. Property in Norfolk was relatively cheaper so we managed to put some money away and altogether our retirement plans came together very well.

In 1979 the local golf club was owned and maintained by the local council. This meant that I became a member without paying a joining fee. It was soon to be taken over by a private company and from then on members paid an annual subscription fee. The course at Fakenham is very pleasantly situated and in fact is partly intertwined with Fakenham racecourse. This means no golf can be played on race days. Meetings are held about eight times a year so this is not too big a problem in itself but golf balls under horses' feet are not good and care when playing near the race rails was very necessary.

At this time, several elderly golfers decided to form a veterans' golf club. They formed a committee of quite talented people to run this, and the secretary was soon in the process of organising matches against other clubs. In quite a short time we had a strong following of over 50-year-old golfers. It was decided that one had to be over fifty to be a member, so I was able to join this merry band. Although our course at Fakenham was a nine-hole course it was still quite a stern course in terms of difficulty. Thus in order to complete a match against other eighteen-hole course clubs our course had to be played twice. By having different placement of tees it was possible to make the course quite interesting.

The yearly subscription at Fakenham golf course was much lower than that imposed by the more prestigious Norfolk clubs so we had quite a widespread following. Many of the senior golfers were not at all well off and so our small Fakenham club had quite a big talented membership. We played against most of the other clubs in Norfolk both at home matches and away. This meant golfing treats, like playing at Cromer, Sherringham and Hunstanton, all situated on the pleasant North Norfolk coast. The matches were followed by a lunch and this meant dressing up for the occasion. There were after-lunch speeches and other niceties and a match day could probably last from 9am to 3pm which was a very pleasant way of spending a day. Teams were never chosen on merit for these occasions and the captain and secretary gave all members a number of games during the season.

We were quite pleased with our bungalow, it had three fairly large bedrooms and in these early years of retirement we had all three furnished as bedrooms. In those days we seemed to have more visitors as Norfolk is a pleasant place to visit. Later on as our grandchildren grew in numbers we needed the three bedrooms. During our later years here in Fakenham we have found it more convenient to turn one of the bedrooms into a dining room. This leaves us a larger lounge area which we use more as a leisure room than before.

During the early 1980s we had a very nice holiday in Southern Ireland. We flew from Stansted in Essex to Cork and being more sprightly in those days had a good touring holiday interspersed with interesting walks. We hired a car and had about twelve days along the beautiful West Coast and found no difficulty in finding bed and breakfast accommodation. The people we met were very helpful and the food was excellent. They went out of their way to prepare fresh sandwiches, and were very pleasant to get along with.

We arrived one day at Ballybunnion where there is a famous and prestigious golf club. The whole town was festooned with bunting which, alas, was not to welcome us. It seemed that the President of the United States was due there for a reception and a round of golf, hence all the regalia. We did find B and B accommodation there for the night. We were due to retrace our steps the next day and we had the pleasure of driving round the various peninsulas in reverse. The coastal views I remember were really wonderful and altogether we had a holiday to remember.

One project that to me was a necessity was to extend the garage so that I could have a decent-size workshop at the rear. I kept putting this off as at the back of the garage was an oil tank which held a considerable amount of oil for the central heating. The boiler itself was in a cupboard in the kitchen and was never really very efficient, it had an annoying habit of cutting out and when this happened a red light appeared. We had a kind neighbour who frequently helped us to sort this problem out. He was of the opinion that we had inherited a rogue boiler and said that the previous owners had problems with it as well. We persevered with this troublesome appliance for about two years and had had to replace the ignition gadget several times. I suppose we were just unlucky as the said neighbour and others around had no trouble at all with their oil-fired boilers.

Eventually I got fed up with all this and decided to get a local heating engineer to fit a solid fuel fire with a back boiler to replace the oil one. I was thus able to get the large oil tank removed from the back of the garage as part of the deal. This enabled me to build on to the existing garage a brick compartment to hold the solid fuel and also to encompass a good size workshop. As the existing garage had a felt roof I decided to take this off and have a gabled tile roof which covered the whole structure. This proved to be a relatively simple task as I could once again use my limited brickwork skills and established joinery know-how to good effect.

I was very fortunate to get matching tiles at a bargain price. A golfing friend who lived nearby in a village had employed a builder to build him a double garage adjacent to his house. He had got planning permission to do this but when the building inspector came to examine the new structure, my friend was in for a bit of a shock. It appeared that the main house was a listed building and had old clay tiles on the roof. He was told in no uncertain terms that the new roof would have to be tiled to match the house. When my friend told me this, I made him an offer for the tiles that he was going to remove and so I got enough concrete tiles which in fact matched our more modern bungalow, for fifty pence each. So today after our long spell of retirement we are still the only people with a tiled gabled roof garage in the near vicinity which really looks nice. Concrete roof tiles of course are much heavier than clay ones but provided the roof rafters and struts are well proportioned they do the job just as well.

Our first five years of leisure went very well. Jo became heavily involved with the W.I. (Women's Institute) and has been so for all the years of our retirement. She had done the job of secretary and was also president for several years and in the latter years has been responsible for organising speakers for their monthly meetings. By this time I was playing golf about three times a week and in those early days the senior section had matches against the main club members as well as mixed games with the very strong ladies' section. These latter games were pleasant social affairs and quite enjoyable occasions with small trophies for the winners.

From Sixty to Sixty-Five

The garden at 52 North Park, Fakenham was quite large really and encompassed the front, one side and the back area of the property. The other side was occupied by our extended garage and workshop so it was quite a compact unit. It consisted in the main, and still does, of three lawns surrounded by borders or fences. Not being an over-keen gardener I made myself responsible for the grass cutting and Jo kept the borders and bushes under control. A previous owner who was a keen gardener had done most of the hard work and planning of the garden. There were quite a few exotic plants and bushes already in place which made our job more easy. We did put in an area of mixed heather plants that looked very nice in Spring and Autumn and we also added a water feature that embraces a showery arrangement that looks very attractive when switched on.

The town of Fakenham in the early Eighties was very different than it is today. The main employer in the town was a firm called Fakenham Press and their works dominated the centre of the town. The whole setup seemed to me to be a relaxed one and not over competitive. I say this because I played golf with some of their employees and also some of their retired ex-staff. For several years I also played bridge with three of their workers and we belonged to the King's Lynn Bridge Club. We shared cars on these occasions which worked out very well and we met fairly regularly twice a week on Mondays and Thursdays. From getting to know these people well I got the impression that the staff generally abused their employers and took liberties such as private phone calls and using firm's materials as their own. We played Bridge at King's Lynn for about five years and as the club was quite a large one the competition was quite fierce but friendly. Being a large town

156

it was quite normal to have as many as twenty tables on Bridge evenings and they had three divisions, similar to those in football, so the players were in a position to strive for promotion and avoid relegation.

Inevitably the firm of Fakenham Press collapsed like a house of cards. This would have been in the mid-1980s and came as a great shock to all the complacent employees. All the working ones that I knew had difficulty in getting new jobs, and the married pair that I played Bridge with went as far away as Hayling Island in Hampshire to get similar work.

There was certainly great trauma in the town as probably a hundred or more people were affected. Within a few years the tall buildings of Fakenham Press were no more and the site is now relegated to car parks that surround the market area.

I played Bridge at King's Lynn for a further ten years, with a lady partner who lived opposite our bungalow in a large house. Her husband was a bomber pilot in the R.A.F. and in fact was flying the delta-wing nuclear bomber that became a legend of the times. They had two children who were away at boarding school and with him away on his duties I suppose she was rather a lonely person.

We got to know them quite well and had the occasional meal out together when he was on leave. I helped her out with her car problems as they had a Renault 14 at the time which was very similar to our car. I remember on one occasion when she came over at about seven in the morning, saying her car would not start. She was very upset as she was due to pick her husband up at Heathrow Airport in the mid-morning, so she had a problem. It was a frosty winter's morning so I guessed the trouble was due to a run down battery, so I simply took the battery from our car and exchanged it for hers and away she went.

Her husband eventually finished his term as a pilot and he became an air controller at an airfield in Lincolnshire, we were sorry to see them go and of course I was again looking for a Bridge partner.

One of my fellow senior golfers who was named Arthur Loades who lived at King's Lynn was also a member of the bridge club.

We had become quite friendly and often played in golf matches as partners. He normally played his Bridge with his wife as partner but they didn't always get on well at the Bridge table so he asked me to play with him. His golf in fact was much better than his Bridge but because of our friendship I agreed to partner him at Bridge, but in truth was never too happy with this arrangement. He tended to gamble at the game which is not the thing to do. You need a sensible and thoughtful approach to be successful and over the few years we played together we didn't do very well.

Our army son Simon had some influence on our lives at this time in the early 1980s. He was married to his wife Diane by this time and they had a daughter Helen who was about two years old. He was stationed for two spells as part of our forces in Germany and we had two separate holidays staying with them. These were very pleasant breaks for us and as they had a car which Diane drove we were able to get around the country which was nice. I can remember going to the town of Linz and other places along the river Rhine. We visited the Black Forest area as well and I remember being at Koblenz which is near the confluence of the Rhine and Moselle rivers.

Eldest son Peter at this time was happily married to Lyn and lived in a large house in Sussex, not too far away from Christ's Hospital. He was in charge of English and Drama at an independent school nearby and seemed very happy with life. The house was set in a delightful garden which was fairly extensive, they also had a piece of land on the opposite side of the road which they cultivated to some extent as a vegetable plot. I suppose Lyn must have inherited some considerable wealth from her parents as they had quite an affluent lifestyle.

David was also married and lived in central Kent near Faversham. He had by this time joined a high-powered firm based in London, somewhere near the Elephant and Castle area. This firm I believe did work on failing businesses on the same lines as the old 'time and motion' study people. Their aim was to get firms more efficient and I can remember David saying that he was employed on a project concerning the National Health Service. It was to do,

I think, with consultants who, being a law onto themselves, were taking time off to suit themselves rather than their patients. He was in charge of a team and they had to prepare a report to go to the government and I felt at this time the work was very stressful and it showed.

Both Tim and Matthew were still semi-nomadic and lived in the Bristol area. For several years during this period they had a fruit packing contract with a farmer at Upwell, which is a village near the east border of Norfolk not far from Downham Market. It seemed that Tim was in charge and the large mainly apple orchard was turned into a tented camp. There were about a dozen pickers and as the time was late summer there were some children about and it was really a well organised affair. Downham Market, being only thirty miles from Fakenham, meant that we could visit this hive of industry and enjoy a nice cup of tea in the boys' company.

The farmer eventually retired and I believe the orchards were uprooted so the land could be used for normal farming or some other purpose.

Matt had by this time acquired a friend who in later years has become his partner. They eventually moved to Cornwall and still live together. He has a gardening business which keeps him ticking over with steady self-employment. His lady friend Birgit is of German origin but well settled in this country now and has probably taken out naturalisation papers. She has a good job with a housing firm as a sort of trouble-shooter and has passed exams to get into this position.

Whether by coincidence or design Tim decided to live in Norfolk and during our retirement years we have seen more of him than any other member of our family. He had friends that lived in the country village of Wood Dalling which is about ten miles from Fakenham and they allowed him to live on their fairly large and secluded site. He bought a smallish caravan and was able to live quite cheaply. His friends were Rob and Helen Blaydon and for most years they have spent the winter months in India, the actual place was on the south east coast at Goa. Rob is a keen motorcyclist and has several vintage bikes. He also has a Royal Enfield 'Bullet' in India which the locals have built and made by license for many years. These replicas are mass-produced which makes them cheap to buy and very popular with the locals. They are not, I suspect, made to the same high specification as the original 'Bullets' of the Forties and Fifties era in Britain but they serve a useful service I am sure in the job market. Tim soon had a girlfriend in tow and eventually they had a son called Jack. Although Tim had the surname of Nixon and his lady's name was Vicky Ridgeway, they decided to name Jack with the surname of Smiles. This they explained was because he smiled a lot, as babies do.

They decided not to allow Jack a formal schooling, which we thought to be unwise. He had a life of freedom and spent much of it in adult company; this in some way became beneficial as he has turned out to be a delightful person in all respects. I suppose that mixing at school, as children must, promotes bad as well as good traits in a child's mind and as he has grown into adulthood, he has kept the niceties of his upbringing to the fore. He no doubt also lost out as his schooling was narrow and confined, for instance today at his age of twenty three or so he seldom seems to pick up a book to read for pleasure.

Soon after Vicky arrived on the scene she or they purchased a single decker bus and used it for several years as a travelling home, she drove it as at that time Tim was not a driver and they visited music festivals and communes and pursued a semi hippy kind of life.

Tim was quite a good woodworker and they financed themselves for a few years with toy making. I remember they spent hours painting toys and other small craft objects and sold them at craft fairs and other such venues.

It was in the early nineteen eighties that I suffered some kind of nervous breakdown. Even today I cannot explain how this happened, I only remember the facts. First my appetite went and then for several weeks I would not sleep at all and eventually became suicidal.

I remember ending up in a ward in King's Lynn Hospital and feeling really drained. After a day or so I realised that the bulk of the other patients were in really serious conditions, one of them was in a type of enclosed bed and was in some type of drug related disorder. He was like a wild animal and one could not approach his bed safely. There was a young teenage lad who at any time would yell or howl, this went on through the day and night. I enquired, why he was there and a nurse said that his parents were being given a week's respite as they had to endure this noise all the time.

Looking back on that week I suppose it was the nearest I came to being in Bedlam. In that ward there were several patients who were amputees, having lost limbs through severe diabetic disorders. On the Thursday of that week I was moved into a quieter ward and the next day they told me that I could go home.

Our next-door neighbour came in to the hospital to get me. I remember when I left the main ward that a man near the door who had lost parts of both legs saying to me "What I wouldn't give to be walking out of here like you are", this made feel very humble indeed and I suspect somewhat ashamed.

That week in hospital I suppose was meant to be therapeutic and if it was, it worked. It still took me the best part of a year to fully recover. I found driving the car very difficult but I was determined enough to overcome this. I tended to take the car out for quiet country runs which I gradually extended in length.

I can remember doing a journey to see Simon and family who were stationed at Woolwich Military Hospital at the time. To get there I had to drive to the M11, thence via the Dartford tunnel to Woolwich. This I found was a serious test of my driving and mental ability, as I felt quite unwell and stressed. Even when we got there I was still apprehensive about the journey back and didn't really enjoy the stay. Having achieved that visit I suppose I benefitted from that and gradually got better. I still cannot understand how all this happened and I never will. Jo was very good during these awful times as they must have tested her patience. Today in my late eighties I can still drive with confidence and it all seemed such a stupid occurrence in my life, in hindsight.

It was in nineteen eighty-two that I achieved my highlight at bridge. Once a year the club had a singles competition for the "Stanley Rowe" cup. King's Lynn is the only club that holds this type of event; it is not a competition that is easy to run, as the movement at the tables is very complex. What happens is that each player must play with a different partner each time for one hand and it needs a very experienced tournament director to achieve this.

On that evening I suppose things were just meant to go well for me. To win I suppose one needs the right partner and favourable cards plus a bit of luck and on that occasion things came right on the night.

It was very nice to receive this cup at the annual prize giving and I remember Mr Warren the chief tournament director being quite complimentary. For a player in the second division to achieve this was a rare occurrence and he said so. So for one year I held this rather prestigious trophy and I still have a record of the event, which I tend to treasure.

From Sixty-Five to Seventy

This period of my life I expected to be a routine follow on from my first five years and to some extent it was. The golf and bridge went on steadily and Jo was well installed into the W.I. and at the time was busy being President. She and her fellow members often went on week trips and with the regular meetings she was often away. During the Spring and Summer months I was frequently at other golf clubs and with the occasional match to play in I was also often away from home. This worked well as I never felt a neglected husband. This was not the case with all our senior golfers and I often heard the term "golf widow" mentioned.

This fairly nice period in our life was about to be shattered by an event that still clouds over our life. David still had this stressful job and when we were invited to visit him and his wife in Kent, he always seemed to be rushing about. We met him at Victoria station on one occasion and had arranged for him to gather us up so that we could travel to Faversham on the same train. Because the tube trains were crowded he got from his office near the Oval late and I remember that I was collected rapidly out of W.H.Smiths where I was browsing and whizzed along the platform to catch a train. Apparently he had tickets for a performance in Canterbury and it was a question of a quiet meal then a fast trip on the motorway to get to the theatre on time. This was an example of his lifestyle at the time. David was thirty-six years old. His first marriage didn't last too long, I think they disagreed to some extent about having children and decided to part. He married Gill eventually and they moved into a listed thatched house on the outskirts of Faversham. We visited them on several occasions and the area had many attractions including several National Trust houses, so these excursions were very pleasant. When at Cambridge he had been a key rower and had procured a Clare College Oar, which he was very proud of and he had it on exhibition in their garage.

In early July nineteen eighty-six Jo and I had arranged to go on holiday, to visit a nursing friend. The friend was one of the students Jo had trained with at Southend on Sea hospital and several of them kept in touch for many years, This one and her husband lived at Sydney in Gloucestershire on the west side of the river Severn, they were Mary and her husband John Jones. We had visited them before, as that area is a very pleasant one in close proximity to the Forest of Dean and its beauty spots.

Before setting off I had phoned the family to say that we would be away from home for about a week. When I phoned David's number, Gill answered and said that David was unwell and was going into hospital at Canterbury for tests. She advised us to phone again during our holiday as she would know more about David's condition by Thursday of that week so that is what we did.

At the time to add to these problems, Gill and David had had their baby, which was only a few days old. It was a boy and he was named Tom, (not Thomas) after Gill's father. We had been a little surprised when told a few months previously that Gill was pregnant but also very pleased at them having a family.

When I phoned Gill as arranged on that Thursday I was told the shocking news that David had severe cancer problems and only had a few weeks to live. It was really devastating and took quite a while for this news to register. Although it appeared that nothing at all could be done to help, we decided to come home the next day and it was a terrible journey.

We got down to see David in the hospital on two occasions, which of course were very sad events. He had many friends from his work who visited as well but inevitably he died and it seemed such a waste of a good human person.

Jo and I went to the funeral with Simon and his family who were still at Woolwich. They had a large people carrier so it was convenient together. My sister Doreen who had looked after David as a child was there and Tim and Vicky also arrived unexpectedly.

Peter and Lyn came back with us to Gill's house I remember as the sad day was over.

A few weeks later the urn containing David's ashes was interred in the churchyard at Faversham church and again we had a family gathering.

My sister Doreen had always shown a keen interest in David's life and welfare and just before she died a few years ago she sent me a snapshot of a four-year-old David in a silver frame. We also have other photographs of him and he is seldom out of our thoughts.

We have seen Tom grow up and to a great extent he has filled the void in our lives.

Simon and Diane also gave his name to their youngest son, which was nice, they have four children now, two girls and two boys.

One of the main attractions about Norfolk of course is the coastline as there are so many large and small places to visit. It has always been very popular with birdwatchers but in recent years as holidays overseas have become more expensive it has become quite tourist orientated as well. We have certainly enjoyed driving the coastal road on numerous occasions and never tire of the sea and the flats that encourage all the wildlife, especially the birds.

During our many years of retirement here we have been in the habit of going out for lunch on Fridays. Early on we tried out many pubs both inland and on the coast and it was fun exploring the many lesser known villages. We have in recent years tended to go to favourite places where we know we can get good service including a decent pint. This I suppose would seem an extravagance to some people but Jo cooks and prepares meals on the other five days and this has become a treat that we both enjoy. We have also got to know Norfolk very well and I just feel we deserve a little pampering as we certainly worked hard during our lives, so why not?

One of the changes I made to the bungalow in the early eighties was to enlarge the lounge window that looks over the rear garden. This meant removing the under window radiator and putting a long slim one in its place, thus allowing me to lower the window by two feet. I hired a special disc cutter to cut neatly through the

165

brickwork, which enabled me to remove the required number of brick courses. The existing window was then removed and the larger window frame was made and fitted. This sounds and was a simple and straightforward job but overall it took about a week to complete. At nights I covered the opening so that any intruder would have problems getting over my recumbent form. The window, as it still is today, consisted of a large double glazed pane with no hinged openings. This measured seven foot wide by six foot high approximately and I measured this opening very carefully and set off to the glaziers in Dereham. They agreed to make the pane as required but insisted on coming out and measuring the aperture themselves and setting it in place. I suppose that was sensible enough as they took on the responsibility. The pane would certainly have been very heavy so in all they did a very good job. So we have a super picture window that allows us to see our garden all year round and as we have a good variety of bird life that is just great! On two occasions we have had a sparrow hawk on the lawn, which had landed on and devoured a smaller bird. A grisly affair but an unusual and rare thing to see.

During Simon's long spell in the army which was about thirty years we, Jo and I had another holiday treat. He and his family were stationed in Hong Kong and we were invited out to stay with them for a whole month. The long flight out there was free to us, as parents of a serving soldier and as we stayed with them too accommodation also cost us nothing. We had a wonderful month out there and a holiday that under normal circumstances we would not have been able to afford. Simon and Diane, because they had been out there for a long period, knew the place quite well and we benefited from that. We were able to buy discounted goods, particularly clothes, and we also got to know a jeweller who was well known to army personnel and we got some good bargains from that firm.

The city itself on both sides of the river was so clean and tidy. The underground system was spotless and this really stood out when compared with the tube system here at home. The seats in the trains were made from stainless steel and were moulded to fit the human form and very comfortable.

There were quite a number of typhoon warnings while we were out there but nothing serious occurred except that the high winds seemed to be dangerous. Many of the dwellings were high-rise as in most modern cities and the flat that the family lived in was on a top floor. The landing ground for the aircraft was near by, and aircraft came very close to the rooftops when landing. This could be quite frightening and at times one wondered if there were tyre marks on the roof.

Jo and I went on several excursions while we were in Hong Kong. These were usually organised affairs that tourists could book! We decided to go on an all day trip that took us by riverboat to Macau and this also included a coach journey into China itself. I think we spent the morning in Macau and I remember visiting the plush gambling rooms, which are a well-known feature of the place.

When we boarded the coach that would take us over the border into China; an official supported by two armed soldiers gathered up all the passengers' passports and disappeared into the control room. After a considerable time elapse he came out looking very perplexed and angry and make us all get off the coach and line up to be counted. The number of passports was, it appeared one less than the number of people and so into the control room he went again. The fault of course was all down to us, the Nixons and eventually he stomped toward us, soldiers in abeyance, gesticulating as to why we hadn't pointed out that we had a dual passport. Well, eventually we were allowed on our way with us looking rather sheepish.

The trip into China was itself quite an experience. It was apparent that we were only allowed to see what the Chinese wanted us to see. I am sure that the visit to one of the villages was well prepared. We were allowed to visit the school and the classrooms were really crowded, in fact the teacher was in such a small area that he was almost clamped to the blackboard. The pupils seemed very studious and I imagine thought themselves lucky to be there at all.

Quite close to the border, and much to our surprise we were shown a golf course that had been laid out or designed by Arnold

Palmer, the very famous American golfer. So there is change going on in China. We also saw coolie types of worker with their traditional hats and clothes irrigating the fields with shoulder supports attached to buckets. Until that day I hadn't realised that pineapples grew in the ground like sugar beet but had thought they grew on trees, so we did get some educational benefit from the trip.

There was an island on the river that the army used as a holiday camp where personnel could go with their families for a break. It was called "Woodcutters Island" and while we were there Simon and Diane and their two young daughters, Helen and Louise, went to stay for a few days, and we were also invited. We stayed several days and had an opportunity to explore the island. Quite unexpectedly, in the middle of the night we were all hauled out of bed and had to return to the mainland because a hurricane, which had a severe high possibility of danger had been forecast. It all seemed so dramatic at the time as river transport had to be organised and everything seemed so frantic. It all turned out to be futile as nothing happened but procedure by the military had to be observed at all costs.

Our pleasant memories of that holiday are still with us and we still have souvenirs of the event. The whole place reeked of have and have-nots as the poorer areas were there in abundance. We still remember the "bag ladies" who roamed the streets, making a living on dust bin contents, for them it seemed a way of life but to see these elderly women getting a living off the streets seemed awful.

One other momentous occasion was our visit to the Peak. We were booked in to have a meal at the restaurant at the top but the ride to get there was really unforgettable. It was by a type of funicular railway and was so steep that if you looked out of the carriage window everything looked considerably out of perpendicular. It was a sensation difficult to describe but something I have not experienced before or since and feel that I never will.

Coming home was rather an anti-climax and in some ways seemed like a dream. Everything was a bit mundane but we had to settle down to our usual Norfolk routine. Thinking about it, we have both lived a very busy retirement and I suppose that is just in our nature.

From Seventy to Seventy-Five

One of the things that I had hoped to do in my early retirement was to make a stringed instrument such as a violin. I suddenly realised, as I passed my seventieth birthday that if I wanted to realise this ambition, I would have to get on with it quickly. I obtained two books on the subject to study, as I knew that instrument making was a specialised subject and skill. One of the books which Peter and Lyn gave us as a Christmas present was a very comprehensive one, which was based on the instruments of Stradivarius and this I found most useful. The other book had more of a historical flavour and was more of a good read.

When I obtained a catalogue of materials from a good supplier I realised that because of the expense that would be involved it would be wise to get some practical tuition and to this end I approached a violin-maker who lived in Buxton which is about five miles from Fakenham. I arranged to have a series of four-hour sessions over ten weeks mainly to absorb the techniques and also to know about the specialist tools required.

The man was named Dominic Excell and he was obviously a skilled maker with a diploma in instrument making from the "Newark School of Violin Making". He was very helpful and allowed me to borrow a template with which to make a mould so that I could get started on producing an instrument in my workshop at home.

At this time he was in fact, struggling to make a living and was also having domestic problems. I suppose that with modern music such as rock and pop the call for the more classical instruments was on the wane. He was having to spend his time more on repairing than making; some of the cellos he worked on had badly splintered fronts and the re-creation work was very painstaking and tedious. This work was also difficult to price and altogether he was not happy with his lot. He often asked me if I would pay him in cash at the end of a morning's tuition and it seems a shame that such a talented person should be in such dire straits.

Still this was hardly my affair and I was certainly getting good value from these lessons. As I progressed with my first violin he was always prepared to loan me special tools and clamps over a weekend, which helped me a great deal. We became quite good friends over the few years that I knew him but eventually his marriage failed and he went to America to try out his skills there.

I had established quite a good rapport with a firm of suppliers in Birmingham called "Sydney Evans and Son". The materials they supplied were of the highest quality and they were quick to supply. Over the ten years that I made instruments I got to know the son, David who by this time ran the firm quite well. This was only by phone but as our business progressed he would give me discounts on various components such as finger boards, strings and bridges. He knew he could always rely on me for quick payment and so we got on well. This apparently was not so with many of his customers and to my surprise the firm folded in 1990 and this was quite a shock to me and a blow to him. When he told me this was happening he was trying to sell off his existing stock and offered me, as a good customer the whole requirements for making a cello at twenty five percent off. This included all the special parts such as string adjusters; in fact everything needed to complete a fine cello.

Having made a cello in the mid nineties I had not really intended to make another but this was too good a bargain to resist so I succumbed to the temptation. In fact I decided to buy a set of drawings from a well known American firm for a 7/8 size instrument and I must say that I really enjoyed making it.

From 1991 to 2001 I succeeded in making one stringed instrument each year. The plan was to start making about September with a view to completing it by June thus allowing three months to get the varnishing done. Good weather and selected sunny days was essential to complete the job properly. This of course included the clear primary coats and the process was altogether very demanding as many months of good work could be ruined by one carelessly applied coat.

The outlay to get started was quite heavy when my tuition expenses were added to the cost of materials, nevertheless I had caught the bug and decided on my one yearly project of doing an instrument as above.

About 1993 I went to the town of Downham Market to a specialist tool supplier to get a particular wood gauge I needed. This place turned out to be situated in the old cinema and their business was mainly to do with carving tools and lathes and relevant materials. A youngish man was demonstrating lathe techniques to a customer when I arrived so an older customer served me. He had apparently handed over the business to the son who had transformed and modernised it.

In this old cinema I noticed that the tiers where the seats had been were stocked with boards of hardwood most of which appeared to have been there for years and were covered in dust and muck. I asked the elderly man if by chance there were any maple boards among them and he said it was very doubtful as the business in his day had been in furniture making and maple of course was not a popular wood for that purpose. Then after some thought he said that right at the top there might be the odd board but he assured me that it would only be very plain grained and ordinary. He said I was welcome to go and look which I did but it was difficult to know where as the whole area was so disordered. He however, suddenly appeared after reluctantly climbing the stairway and eventually found what he was looking for. This turned out to be two short scruffy looking boards still with the ancient bark on the edges. They were obviously very old and he reckoned them to be in the region of ninety years and dated from his father's time. The boards on examination were just about thick enough for a violin back and I thought with care I might get enough for one complete back from each board. This man being old and wise had by now worked out what I wanted the boards for and surprised me by saying, "let him (meaning the son) think you are buying two scruffy old boards otherwise he will overcharge you". When we got down below and into the good light I decided to buy the boards and the price would be fifteen pounds, which I bargained down to twelve pounds and so I departed.

The two violins that I made using this old maple, turned out to be the best sounding ones that I made. One that I still have, at my very old age was played by the leader of the Norfolk Symphony Orchestra and she said it compared with her instrument very favourably and in fact was quite amazed. The appearance of these backs was indeed very plain compared with the high flame wood that I had bought from Sydney Evans over the years but after all it is the sound emitted from the instrument that is important.

The second instrument with this plain wood I sold in rather strange circumstances.

We had had a visit from Jean who was my brother Lesley's daughter. She had married a person who had emigrated to Australia many years before and they had been back to Northern Ireland to visit their parents. It happened that a friend of her husband's was in charge of a religious group that were situated at Taverham near Norwich. I think the church was called the "Church of the Proclaimers" and did good works in the backward areas of Africa. The man in charge must have been some form of Lay preacher but he was also very wealthy and owned the car franchise of BMW in Norwich.

Jean and her husband had been invited to stay for a week at this church and while there, contacted us and we invited them to Fakenham to lunch with us. Being an amateur woodworker himself her husband John was very interested in my violin making and it must have impressed him quite considerably.

It seemed that at the church, that people gathered round the meal table, and gave short off the cuff speeches and he quite spontaneously gave a short dissertation on my efforts.

Well, a few weeks after they had departed back to Australia I had a phone call from a lady. She wanted to know if I had available a violin for sale? I told her that I had three instruments that she could try out and we arranged for her to come to our bungalow to do this. It turned out that she was a member of the congregation at this church and had been impressed with John's speech. She wanted an instrument as a present for her daughter who was about to start a University course.

The strange thing was that she had apparently approached my friend Dominic Excell enquiring the price of a new violin and he had quoted her a price of £3000 for one from stock or £3,500 for an instrument made to order. The latter option would take about six months and she would be required to pay a £1000 deposit. The lady in question, although a competent violinist herself was in fact a piano teacher and her name was Mrs A Thomas and she lived in Fakenham. Piano tuition was her main source of income so she was not a wealthy person.

When she came to play my instruments, to my surprise she brought in a violin that had been given to her when she was 21 years old by her parents as a coming of age present. It was in a very sorry state especially the front, which was badly cracked. The back and bouts (sides) were in good condition and it had the "William Hill" stamp on it, which indicated that it was of good vintage. The case it was in was hardly recognisable as a case at all and showed that the instrument had been through difficult times over the years. The bow needed a new tip and a complete repair but in expert hands I realised that both the violin and bow had value.

She played the three violins I had on offer and chose the old maple back one, which I knew she would and made me an offer for it of £1,300. In addition, I was to have the "Hill" violin and bow as part exchange.

I decided to accept this arrangement as I could use the money to buy subsequent materials for other instruments. At the time I was working on my first cello and I knew that the fittings for it would be expensive, for example a set of cello strings at the time was over a hundred pounds.

This all worked out very well and I volunteered to maintain the instrument that she bought for six months. I knew that as a new instrument some adjustments to the pegs and sound post would be necessary, so this seemed fair to me.

I was in no hurry to tackle the repairs on the "Hills" violin but I did take it to Dominic Excell, who assured me that the violin was well worth repairing. Strangely he offered to buy the bow for one hundred pounds, which I refused. Instead I agreed to let him re-tip and re-hair the bow and would pay him fifty pounds for doing this. When I collected the bow a few weeks later it was in pristine condition. He said its value was now about three hundred pounds as all the metal parts were solid silver so I was glad that I had not parted with it for his crafty one hundred pounds offer.

About six months later I had a phone call from Dominic with an offer for the "Hills" violin. It appeared that his latest student was a Korean who wanted tuition in instrument repairs. He also wanted an instrument for his daughter and Dominic thought that this accredited violin would fit the bill if I would part with it. As I hadn't the specialised equipment needed to repair the cracks or perhaps the skill needed for this very delicate work, I decided to accept this offer for £800 pounds. I suspect that Dominic charged the Korean gentleman much more but overall I had done pretty well with my deal with Mrs Thomas.

While I still had contact with Dominic I decided to make a viola. He suggested that I make a larger model than standard, as these were quite rare. He had a suitable template for the body, which he allowed me to copy and I was soon occupied in making a 16½" model. This involved exactly the same methods as constructing a violin but all the measurements were of course different, including the thicknessing of the back and front. I enjoyed making this and it turned out well, I still have it in a display cabinet with the other instruments that I have made.

Roundabout my seventy fifth birthday I decided to make a lute and this proved to be quite a challenge. I bought a set of drawings and a booklet from "The Lute Society" publications, as this was essential. The seven pieces that formed the back were of equal thickness all over which made the construction of the bowl or back a little easier. These pieces, however in shape were quite complicated to make and had to be fitted very accurately onto a former. This required infinite patience as these pieces being steam bent had to be glued together. They were only 2mm thick so this was quite a problem; the inside of the joint was reinforced with strips of calico glued to the inside of the bowl. The other problem that I found was difficult was cutting out the decorative fret on the pine front. The wood being so much softer than the maple back was difficult to cut accurately even with a machine fret saw and I was not too happy with the final result.

The rest of the structure was more straightforward but still required care, skill and above all patience.

The back pieces of maple I had been fortunate enough to buy from Dominic Excell and although the wood was highly flamed and therefore very attractive, this also meant brittleness, which made bending more of a problem.

When I had completed making the lute I made intensive enquiries about getting someone to play it. The lute as an instrument is not that popular in this day and age and of course has its origins more in medieval times.

Eventually, while buying a CD from a classical music shop in the Norfolk town of Holt, when enquiring hopefully the proprietor said he knew of a guitarist who also played the lute. It turned out that this man lived quite close to Fakenham and when I contacted him agreed to play my lute for me. It turned out that I had two pairs of strings in the wrong order, which had to be rectified before he played so he agreed to come at a later date. When he came again he was able to play the lute and to me it sounded great. We made a tape recording, which I still have of some well-known pieces by J.S.Bach.

He valued the lute at about a thousand pounds and suggested if I wanted to sell it, the best place would be a University town. To do this would mean travelling and also getting a suitable case for its protection. I decided that as I enjoyed looking at it and didn't need the money I would keep my lute and still have it!

From Seventy-Five to Eighty

In 1996 I had a rather unexpected honour, as I became golf captain of our seniors section. It wasn't something that I had sought but when asked to stand for election and after all the years of enjoyment that I had had it seemed churlish to refuse. These and many other matters were finalised at our general meeting, which took place in October. That year there were two candidates for the job and I was rather surprised to get many votes and this encouraged me to do the job well. The duration was for one year and meant working in close harmony with the secretary. The matches against other clubs entailed the biggest organisational problem as senior's days came on various days of the week. For instance our day at Fakenham was Tuesdays, so our home games had to be on that day. The main club members had priority in many matters and the seniors' section had little clout and we had to be careful not to tread on various toes. The Ladies section had their golf day on Mondays and also had priorities with the functions and matches. Another complication was race days as the horse racecourse intertwined with the golf course so we also had to be aware of the racing calendar.

During a year we played against fourteen other golf clubs so altogether this meant twenty-eight matches, home and away. These were really very pleasant affairs as we got to visit all the major clubs in Norfolk. We played Royal Cromer for instance but there was never any snobbishness with any clubs, just a lot of elderly gentlemen enjoying a game of golf. We had to dress properly for the dinner after the games and this entailed for my part making twenty-eight dinner speeches. After the first one was over I didn't find this an ordeal, as I had expected, as the atmosphere was just so friendly.

The Fakenham golf course, although a nine hole one is far from easy as there are many hazards for the unwary golfer. The river Wensum borders several of the holes which causes problems and the placement of the many sand traps is also an unseen difficulty. So this provided quite a challenge and the locals could usually hold their own against the long hitters from some of the eighteen hole clubs. We reckoned to win our home games and lose the away ones which seemed fair enough, the competition was always there and the unexpected sometimes happened.

Tim was by now well established as a cabinet-maker and busy making all sorts of articles for friends, family and others. He had got a new partner, Jayne, and they had a daughter, Rachael, born in March 1996. She is a lovely gentle child who often visits with Tim, and helps us, especially Jo, round the house.

Way back in 1954 when I left Broomfield Secondary School I was given two LPs (long playing records), which were among the earliest stereophonic records made. I had asked for the two records as a present and when I went to James Dace's record shop at Chelmsford to choose there was in fact little choice. This was, however, the start of my classical record collection, which I continued with until the early years of my retirement. Over my whole lifetime both Jo and myself have enjoyed listening to the classics and even up to 1966 we had no television, so records were our main evening entertainment. We had moved to Billericay when we bought our first TV and I know the year as one of the reasons for buying it was to see World Cup matches.

Although we thoroughly enjoyed our LP collection, when CDs started to appear, I think in the early eighties, we had no hesitation in getting onto that new generation of music genre. CD seemed to be the answer to storage problems and the new sound technology was there to be had.

One day I just took the plunge and took all our LPs to a record dealer in Norwich who after about an hour's appraisal made me a offer which in truth was ridiculously low. In fact at the end of that day I had converted over two hundred LPs into cash which bought only thirteen CDs. Well I can't say that I lost much sleep over this and we had the nucleus of a new collection which I have added to ever since.

In 1997 I saw an advertisement in the library about music theory classes which were to be held at the Fakenham Junior School on Saturday mornings. I decided to go along at the appropriate time 12 noon and a lady was just finishing teaching a group of young children who had joined her class that morning at 11.30am.

It was her suggestion that I didn't join in with this band of noisy youngsters but had a lesson at noon each Saturday, and it appeared that I would be alone which suited me. On the first day I was started on the same course as them as I had no previous knowledge of the subject. Having plenty of spare time I found that I could cope with several consecutive lessons at a time and from September to Christmas I had covered the work leading up to Grade I quite comfortably. She then suggested that I skip Grade 1 and go on to Grade II and take the examination in June.

I found the work very interesting and quite enjoyable, learning the Italian words of description came hardest to me but by sticking to the task I felt ready to take Grade II in June. I managed to get 85%, which was quite creditable, and I felt pleased with myself.

When I renewed the challenge in September 1998 it became a repeat performance really as I skipped Grade III and went on to Grade IV in the June of that year. I didn't do quite as well but still got a certificate with 82% on it.

That September when I went to enrol to do Grade V the lady who had previously taught said her husband took all the grades above four. I found myself doing grade V with a youngish girl who was quite an advanced flautist. She had grade five already as a player but in order to progress with her practical work she needed Grade V theory in a hurry.

The husband who was a very good brass musician was having health problems which in fact had already put paid to his career as he was on the list for heart surgery. So at the first theory lesson he said it would be better for me to aim for the March exam and take it together with the young talented student.

The truth is that as the term progressed I found it much more difficult to work with him as he seemed to have less patience and really I didn't want to be hurried, as it was a pleasure experience for me and not a race. He was probably worried about his health and this could have been a factor. After a few weeks and just before Christmas the young flautist brought along several past Grade V theory papers that she had taken at school where she was getting her main tuition and she had acquired over 90% for all of them, so she was already up and running to do the examination in March. Reluctantly I decided to pull out, I still feel sure that I could have got Grade V if the lady teacher had been my tutor and that I would have worked in a more steady fashion.

When I completed my first cello, I took it along to Dominic so that he could run his eye over it. He was quite impressed really and he suggested that I should get a good cellist to play it. He himself was a competent violinist and played one of his own instruments, in the Norfolk Orchestra. The next time I saw him he gave me the name and phone number of the lady who led the cellos in the orchestra and said she was a sympathetic lady who taught in the local school. He thought it worth my while to see if she would play the cello for me.

As it turned out she taught pupils at Fakenham High School and on Tuesdays she had one or two students for lessons after school hours and she kindly consented to come after these lessons.

When she arrived, the school being only a few minutes from where we lived, she looked a bit tired and frazzled so we offered her tea and a scone while I got my cello laid out on our dining room table. We did one or two adjustments and she then tuned it and suggested she play it in the lounge so that Jo could hear it as well. She made one or two helpful criticisms but on the whole the instrument played very well. She suggested that I should refine the neck by reducing the thickness a little and she also said that the finger board was slightly too wide. This she said made playing easier but a professional cellist would fault it.

The remark about playing prompted me to ask her if she would consider giving me lessons on it. She looked very dubious about this, but I pointed out that my fingers were still very supple at seventy five and because I had studied the theory of music I would like to try. We compromised as she said that I could have seven lessons and at the end of that session, we would make a judgement as to my prospects. Well I carried on with the lessons for over four years and I still enjoy playing. I think in some ways she enjoyed coming round for a relaxing cup of tea after the sometimes stressful battle she had with pupils who didn't practice.

We became quite friendly and we went to the Norfolk Symphony Orchestra Concerts for several years and she would always greet us in the foyer of the Guild Hall where the concerts were held.

She eventually was transferred to more local schools around King's Lynn and this meant a round trip of about 52 miles. I suppose I had also reached the limit of my capabilities so lessons ceased. I still play the cello two or three times a week, and so I have been able to maintain a reasonable standard of playing. The lady's name was Jessica Berners and she still leads the cello section in the orchestra and I feel grateful for her tuition and patience.

From Eighty to Eighty-Five

Roundabout my seventy ninth, or eightieth birthdays I began to feel that eighteen holes of golf was too much for me. By the fifteenth hole I was beginning to flag. A fellow golfer who was not actually a senior, but nearly so, had bought a single-seater, electric, ride on trolley. One day I jokingly asked him if I could try it out for a couple of rounds of golf and he agreed. I knew him quite well as he had owned a plumbing business and had installed our coke fired central heating. This was spring time and the weather was usually fine and I found using this trolley quite a boon. He said he had bought it wholesale from the professional at the Royal Norfolk golf club at Norwich and I suppose it was some trade deal. He said that if I mentioned his name I could get a similar deal, if I needed to buy one. The pro at the Royal Norfolk, it turned out, had been a member of the Fakenham club, when he was younger and he had graduated through some coaching school. He had to be a good player to hold such a prestigious position and when I phoned him to get a price for a new trolley and told him that I was a Fakenham member he gave me a good deal. He said I could have two hundred pounds off the net price and he would also give me two dozen new balls.

So from that time and to my enforced leaving of golf I had transport. This buggy was quite heavy as the batteries had to be 24 volt and on their own were heavy to lift. At first another golfer with whom I was quite friendly would come to the bungalow to help me lift the four units into the hatchback car that I had and then came the problem of getting them off and assembling; this proved to be a real nuisance and so a bit of ingenuity was needed to solve the problem. I found that with the rear seats folded I could fit a raised floor in the back section of the car. The trolley would also fit into

182

the back part when fully assembled so the problem then was to devise a folding ramp system that could be carried so as to roll the trolley off again. By careful measuring and hingeing I was able to do this with a two board system; and the whole thing worked really well and I could do it all by myself.

That was one snag overcome but unfortunately there was another which was not so easy to solve. I had noticed that I was beginning to feel very cold, almost like a fall in body temperature and when winter came, sitting on a trolley on frosty or cold days was a problem. I think now and looking back, this was the beginning of my gradual problem with kidney failure and eventually I had to give up winter golf. Still the trolley served me well enough for about four years and kept me going. I often took it to other clubs for our days out so it did sterling service.

Over the past twenty years I have endeavoured to play Bridge once a week but when it came about that I could no longer play golf, I decided to play bridge twice weekly. My main partner since losing my fellow players from the Fakenham Press days, has been a lady who's early life was in Rhodesia, as it was then. She had her family out there but when her husband died in the Smith era, she decided to come back to England. We met in fact in the early days of the Fakenham bridge club and were almost founder members in the late nineteen eighties. We have played as partners almost continually since then and played for a few years at the local clubs of Swaffham and Holt. When I decided to play on Thursdays as well as Mondays at the local Fakenham club I was asked if I would partner another special lady. She was a very agile minded player of ninety one years old who was undoubtedly a player of some renown. I agreed to play with her with some trepidation, as she was inclined, so I believed, to play her bridge strictly by the book. So we had a trial period (at least it was for me), as I thought that my more unorthodox approach to bridge would not harmonise with her purist one but in fact we have been quite successful as a partnership We are still playing together after about four years and that speaks for itself. When I recently added our combined ages, we are certainly lucky to have retained our mental abilities to reach ripe old ages!

Throughout my lifetime, there has always been two political parties that have been wholly dominant. These have see sawed for power over the years with almost systematic regularity and this proves to me how fickle the human mind is.

What decided me as quite a young person to always vote Labour came about when my family worked for farmer Leslie Drage at New Buildings Farm near Great Chishill.

I could see quite well, that we were reasonably well off regarding food as we lived it and produced it in many ways. The amount of combined effort on our part, however undoubtedly made the farmer and his family really rich and with quite a lavish lifestyle. They dressed well, had riding horses, a posh new car and so on.

One thing that niggled me even at that age was the fact that the son who was my age took the exam for County School at Cambridge and failed to get a place. So indulgent parents were able to send him to an independent private school. On the other hand I strove to pass an exam for a day trade school and although successful up to a point, I could still only look forward to a life of toil. Another very annoying thing that happened was that on polling days during elections, my parents and elder brothers were taken by car to the booths, with strict instructions to vote Conservative. How about that!

In spite of my political leanings I tried to keep out of arguments among fellow colleagues and those often got out of hand. These disputes I remember often cropped up among the soldiers during my army turn and were often unpleasant to listen to.

In all fairness I can remember that during the term of office of Harold Macmillan there was a slogan that said "You have never had it so good", and that was very true. This was particularly noticeable in Education as materials were in very ready supply and with more variety. This to my idea did lead to a certain wastage of commodities and that time of good measure did not last. There certainly was a real good factor to life, during Mr Macmillan's premiership but like most good things it seems had to come to an end.

As with many young children for the first ten years of life we had no religious training at all, except perhaps at school. When we reached our period at Great Chishill this was about to change. At times it meant attending morning and evening services as well as Sunday school. Thinking about those days, I suppose that Sundays were the only times that our parents would get a quiet time together. My sister and I certainly had an abundance of worship at the time that didn't go down too well.

I suppose that my attitude toward religion has been similar to that of my politics. Many times I have heard heavy vocal arguments where people with different beliefs have hammered away at each other.

My instincts say that Mr Darwin's theories are most likely but at the same time if individuals get comfort from their beliefs that is fine by me and fine for them.

In two thousand and six when I had reached the age of 85 years Jo's repeated nagging prompted me to have a blood test at the local surgery. Her nursing skills over our declining years have in an obscure way helped our survival so eventually I went to get this test. She said I looked anaemic and I must admit that I felt very cold at times and was getting some itchiness, as well as being unusually tired. These symptoms I thought just come with advanced age so I was surprised when the blood test was unsatisfactory. The doctor who we usually saw phoned after surgery telling me to see him at 9.00am the next day. It was unusual to get a home phone from our doctors, as at the time it was often several days before you could get an appointment for any ailment.

He didn't beat about the bush and said quite bluntly that I had kidney failure giving me the impression that I wasn't going to last very long.

I had a golfing friend who had been on dialysis at home for several years and was never very well so I was naturally worried. So when I started to write this account I was not too hopeful that I would finish it; but it gave me a challenge I suppose.

Epilogue

From Eighty-Five onwards

In spite of my kidney problems I have now reached the age of eighty eight years. I am not at all sure why as my regular visits to the Renal Unit at King's Lynn Hospital have shown some deterioration each time I have been! I just feel unwell and tired on some days but better on others.

I feel lucky to have reached this age and am determined to die of old age and not kidney failure and this in fact I have already achieved.

All through life a thinking person must feel panic pangs about their eventual demise and this has been true for me. When younger they quickly pass off and later in life you just hope the next day will follow and you are thankful for it when it does.

I still play bridge twice a week but there are times when I don't want to go. Not letting my partner down is a driving force but on these occasions I have had to phone to put a session off.

Learning and listening to music is something that I enjoy and I endeavour to play my cello twice a week which is still satisfying. My fingers have retained their suppleness well and this I believe is because I have always used them in a practical sense.

Any form of hard work or anything that requires constant bending down I cannot do. On Sunday mornings I help Jo out by doing the hoovering and I have to accomplish this by stages.

Another bonus is that I can still drive, this makes hospital visits more easy and I just hope this continues.

We still manage to go out for pub lunches on Fridays and have done this throughout our retirement.

I am writing this while on holiday in Suffolk where we are staying for a week in a hotel in the beautiful village of Lavenham. We managed to get here by careful driving and have been out on sight seeing visits everyday. We plan to go home via Cambridgeshire, as a route, to visit friends and stay for our last night in a hotel in Ely. This will be our main holiday this year as Jo is reluctant to fly and has developed a phobia about escalators and aerodromes. Onward?